Table of Contents

Lecture Outlines for Note Taking

for

Nairne's

Psychology
Fourth Edition

Michelle Miller
Northern Arizona University

THOMSON
WADSWORTH

Australia • Brazil • Canada • Mexico • Singapore • Spain • United Kingdom • United States

Printed in the United States of America

1 2 3 4 5 6 7 09 08 07 06 05

Printer: Thomson West

ISBN 0-495-03163-1

Cover Image: © Workbookstock

Thomson Higher Education
10 Davis Drive
Belmont, CA 94002-3098
USA

For more information about our products, contact us at:
Thomson Learning Academic Resource Center
1-800-423-0563

For permission to use material from this text or product, submit a request online at
http://www.thomsonrights.com.
Any additional questions about permissions can be submitted by email to **thomsonrights@thomson.com.**

Chapter 1: An Introduction to Psychology

Chapter 1: An Introduction to Psychology

_____

_____

_____

_____

_____

_____

_____

Welcome to the Study of Psychology!
- What do psychologists study these days?
  - Normal behavior: causes and mechanisms
– Abnormal behavior and mental illness
- Goals of modern psychology
  - Study the "essentials of behavior and mind"
- Why do people act, think, and feel the way they do?
  - Develop a knowledge base about human and animal behavior

Can Psychology Be Truly Scientific?
- Human behavior difficult to predict precisely
  - However: Governed by general principles
  - Similar to general principles in physics
- Behavior multiply determined
  - Current environment
  - Culture
  - Genetics
  - Moment-to-moment experiences

_____

_____

_____

_____

_____

_____

_____

_____

_____

_____

_____

1

What's it For?
- Goal: Survive in your environment
- Mental processes contribute to survival
- Solving adaptive problems = Find a way to meet challenges to survival
  - Example: How do you recognize and avoid danger?
- Understanding purpose of processes leads to better understanding of those processes

Defining and Describing Psychology: Learning Goals
- Understanding the Modern Definition of Psychology
- Distinguishing among Clinical, Applied, and Research Psychologists

Definition of Psychology
- Root word: "Psyche" = Soul or breath (Greek)
- Scientific study of behavior and the mind
  - Scientific: Based on observation
  - Behavior: Observable actions
  - Mind: Subjective experiences such as thoughts, emotions

What Do Psychologists Do?
- Clinical psychologists
- Applied psychologists
- Research psychologists

_____

_____

_____

_____

_____

_____

_____

Clinical Psychologists
- Main focus: Diagnosing and treating psychological problems
    - Clinics, private practice
- Counseling psychologists
    - Focus on specific adjustment issues, e.g., marriage problems
- Psychiatrists
    - Medical doctors specializing in psychological problems

_____

_____

_____

_____

_____

_____

Applied Psychologists
- Not involved with psychological disorders
- Main focus: Applying psychology to practical problems in the real world
- Examples:
    - School psychologists
    - Industrial/organizational psychologists
    - Human factors psychologists

_____

_____

_____

_____

_____

Research Psychologists
- Main focus: Conducting experiments
- Work in universities, colleges, research institutes
- Specialties:
  - Biopsychologists
  - Personality psychologists
  - Cognitive psychologists
  - Developmental psychologists
  - Social psychologists

Psychological Thought: A Brief History
- The mind-body problem
- The origins of knowledge
- Early schools of thought
  - Structuralism
  - Functionalism
  - Behaviorism
- Freud and the humanists
- The contributions of women

Mind and Body
- Descartes: Two separate entities
  - Mind controls body through pineal gland
  - If so: Impossible to scientifically study the mind
- Psychologists today: One and the same
  - Mind arises from brain activity
  - "The mind is what the brain does" - S. Pinker

Nature vs. Nurture: Where Does Knowledge Come From?

- To what degree are we shaped by innate/inherited tendencies, environment?
- Nativism: Babies are born with a set mental structure, knowing certain things
  - Kant: Inborn mental "structure"
  - Natural selection for certain adaptive traits (Darwin)
  - But: How to distinguish from effects of environment?

The Modern View: Nature Via Nurture

- Many characteristics do have a genetic (inherited) component
  - Examples: Intelligence, personality
- Experience shapes how these characteristics develop
  - Example: Educational experiences
- In other words: Both matter

The First Psychology Laboratory

- 1879, University of Lepzig
- Wilhelm Wundt
  - Philosophy professor with background in physiology
  - Advocated scientific techniques for studying mental processes
  - Main focus: Immediate conscious experience

_____
_____
_____
_____
_____
_____

_____
_____
_____
_____
_____
_____

_____
_____
_____
_____
_____
_____

Structuralism
- Wundt, later Edward Titchener
- Analyze elements of sensations and feelings
    - Example: Sensation of taste is made up of salty, bitter, sour, and sweet
- Technique: Systematic introspection
    - Self-report by trained individuals

_____

_____

_____

_____

_____

_____

_____

Functionalism
- William James, James Rowland Angell
- Understand mental processes by understanding the goal or purpose of those processes
    - Example: What is the goal or purpose of memory?
- Greatly influenced by work of Darwin
    - Adaptive value of mental processes

_____

_____

_____

_____

_____

_____

Behaviorism
- John B. Watson, B. F. Skinner
- Problems with introspection:
    - Cannot directly observe mental events
    - Subjective, varies by individual
- Solution: Focus only on observable behavior in carefully controlled experiments
    - Special emphasis on animal behavior

_____

_____

_____

_____

_____

Sigmund Freud

- Trained as a medical doctor in Vienna
- Observation: Some physical problems have psychological causes
- Established early methods for treating psychological disorders

_____

_____

_____

_____

_____

_____

Freud's Ideas

- Psychoanalysis: Freud's theory of how the mind works and how to address disorders
- Psychological problems solved through insight
- Unconscious mind
  - Conflicts, memories outside of awareness
  - Many psychological problems arise from childhood experiences

_____

_____

_____

_____

_____

Humanistic Psychology

- Criticisms of Freudian psychology:
  - Dark, pessimistic view of human nature
  - Dismisses free will, potential for growth
- Humanistic psychology:
  - Abraham Maslow, Carl Rogers
  - Humans have great potential for growth
  - Therapists should encourage this through nonjudgmental support

_____

_____

_____

_____

_____

_____

_____

Early Psychology: The Role of Women
- Mary Calkins
  - Denied admission to Harvard; "guest" graduate student of William James
  - Never officially received Ph.D.
- Margaret Floy Washburn
  - Became American Psychological Association president in 1921
- Helen Thompson Wooley
  - Helped pioneer study of sex differences

The Focus of Modern Psychology: Learning Goals
- Understanding what it means to adopt an eclectic approach
- Understanding the factors that started the cognitive revolution
- Tracing recent developments in biology and evolutionary psychology
- Explaining why psychologists think cultural factors are important determinants of behavior and mind

What Does "Eclectic" Mean?
- Selecting or adopting information from many different sources rather than relying on one perspective
- Clinical psychology: Choose technique according to client preferences, particular problem
- Research psychology: Focus on biological origins of behavior OR just describe it, depending on the circumstance

Factors Behind the Cognitive Revolution
- 1950s: Shift away from behaviorism, back to interest in internal mental processes
- What led up to the cognitive revolution:
  - Better research techniques allowed more objective observation of mental processes
  - Computers became a new way to understand how the mind works

Biological Factors
- New emphasis on linking brain, mind, and behavior
- Modern technology allows us to:
  - Record the activity of brain cells in response to stimuli in the environment
  - Create images of brain activity during different mental processes, psychological states
  - Better understand normal and abnormal brain chemistry

Evolutionary Psychology
- New emphasis on applying Darwin's ideas of natural selection to behavior and the mind
- For example, humans may have evolved to:
  - Learn language
  - Choose certain kinds of mates
  - Behave a certain way in social groups
- Note: Many claims are controversial

Cultural Factors

- New emphasis on how culture shapes the mind and behavior
    - Culture: shared values, customs, beliefs of a group
    - Can be based on ethnicity, race, class, religion, or other factors that define a group
- Influential researcher: Vygotsky
    - How children think depends on social, cultural environment around them

Solving Problems with the Adaptive Mind

- Behavior is multiply determined, but purposeful
- Focus on the adaptive mind brings relevance to abstract topics
    - Example: Attribution theory
    - Think: When do you need to interpret the behavior of others?
- Also: Critical thinking
    - How does a topic relate to an actual survival or practical problem?

Chapter 2: The Tools of Psychological Research

Chapter 2: The Tools of Psychological Research

_____

_____

_____

_____

_____

_____

_____

The Scientific Method
- Recall: Psychology is the <u>scientific</u> study of behavior and mind
- Four main steps of scientific investigation:
  - Observe
  - Detect Regularities
  - Generate Hypothesis
  - Observe
- Also need operational definitions

_____

_____

_____

_____

_____

_____

_____

What's it For? Unlocking the Secrets of Behavior and Mind
- Observing and describing behavior
- Predicting behavior
- Explaining behavior
- Treating participants ethically

_____

_____

_____

_____

_____

_____

Descriptive Research: Learning Goals

- Describe the techniques and goals of descriptive research
- Explain how psychologists conduct naturalistic research
- Discuss the gains and costs of case studies and surveys
- Explain how statistics can summarize and help interpret data
- Describe the purpose of psychological tests

Goals of Descriptive Research

- Goal: Observe and describe behavior
    - Not: Explain causes (we'll get to that later!)
- Concerns:
    - Reactivity
- Did individuals change their normal behavior because they were being observed?
    - External validity
- Do your observations apply to real life?

Techniques of Descriptive Research

- Naturalistic Observation
- Case Studies
- Surveys
- Psychological Tests

Naturalistic Observation

- Record naturally observing behavior in a real-life situation (not a laboratory)
  - Example: Observe children playing at a day-care center
- Can reduce reactivity by:
  - Participant observation: Blending into the group
  - Measure behavior indirectly

Case Studies

- Focus on a single case, usually an individual
  - Usually involves gathering a lot of information on background, behavior of that individual
- Potential problems:
  - External validity: Is that one individual representative?
  - Verification: How do you know that one individual is being truthful?

Surveys

- Gather a limited amount of information from many people
  - Often, but not always, in the form of a questionnaire
- Potential problems:
  - Obtaining a representative sample of participants
  - Can't obtain in-depth information
  - Are respondents' answers accurate?

Sampling from a Population
- Population: The group the researcher wants to learn about
  - Example: United States residents
- Sample: The subset of the population who participate in the survey
- Random sampling: Everyone in population has an equal chance of being selected
  - Often difficult, but best for ensuring a representative sample

Psyhological Tests
- Tests mainly designed to measure individual differences
- Achievement tests: Measure current level of knowledge or competence in a subject
- Aptitude tests: Measure potential for success in given profession or area of study
- Intelligence tests
- Personality tests

Statistics: Summarizing and Interpreting the Data
- Research projects yield observations (data); researchers attempt to draw conclusions based on the data
- Potential problems:
  - How can you avoid introducing own biases?
  - How do you generalize your findings to a larger population?

Central Tendencies

- Mean: Arithmetic average of a set of scores
  - Summarizes observations into a single representative number
- Mode: Most frequently occurring score in a set of scores
- Median: Middle point in a set of scores
- Median, mode less affected by extreme scores than the mean is

Variability

- Variability: How much the scores in a set differ from one another
  - Example: Two classes might have the same average exam score, but one set of scores might be much more spread out
- Standard deviation: Average distance of scores from the mean
- Range: Difference between the lowest score and the highest score

Inferential Statistics

- Based on laws of probability
- Example: Does a gender difference in scores mean there's a real gender difference in the population?
  - What is the likelihood of getting a difference of a certain size or greater by chance alone?
- Researchers calculate probability that results could have happened by chance
  - Statistical significance

Correlational Research: Learning Goals

- Define correlation and explain how correlations can be used to predict behavior
- Explain why correlations cannot normally be used to determine the cause of behavior

_____

_____

_____

_____

_____

_____

Correlational Research

- <u>Correlation coefficient</u> used to summarize whether two measures vary together
  - Positive correlation: One measure goes up, the other tends to go up as well
  - Negative correlation: One measure goes up, the other tends to go down
  - Zero correlation: Knowing value of one measure does not allow you to predict value of the other measure

_____

_____

_____

_____

_____

_____

_____

Correlations and Causality

- Measures may be correlated, but that doesn't mean one caused the other
  - Example: Does watching violent television cause a child to become aggressive?
- Third variables: A common link that could explain the correlation
  - Example: Perhaps certain kinds of parents allow violent television and encourage aggression

_____

_____

_____

_____

_____

_____

Experimental Research: Learning Goals

- Explain how and why experiments are conducted
- Discuss the difference between independent and dependent variables
- Explain what is meant by experimental control, how it allows for determination of causality

_____
_____
_____
_____
_____
_____

Learning Goals, continued…

- Describe the problems created by expectancies and biases and how these problems are solved
- Discuss the problems associated with generalizing experimental conclusions

_____
_____
_____
_____
_____
_____

Experimental Research: How and Why

- Experimenters actively manipulate environment in order to observe effect on behavior
  - Example: Deliberately expose one group of children to violent show, other group to nonviolent show and observe behavior of each group
- Differs from simply recording, observing behavior

_____
_____
_____
_____
_____
_____

Variables

- Independent variable: Aspect of the environment that is manipulated or changed
    - Must involve at least two conditions
- Example: Violent show / nonviolent show
- Dependent variable: Behavior that is measured or observed
    - Example: Aggressive behavior. Hypothesis tested by observing effect of manipulating independent variable

_____

_____

_____

_____

_____

_____

_____

Experimental Control and Causality

- Experimental group and control group must be similar except with regard to independent variable
- There must be no confounding variables–Confounding variables: Uncontrolled variables that change systematically with the independent variable
- Random assignment: Each participant has equal chance of ending up in any group

_____

_____

_____

_____

_____

_____

Expectancies and Biases

- Participants may guess what the researcher expects to find, change behavior accordingly
- Ways of reducing expectancy effects:
    - Mislead about the purpose of the study
    - Equate expectations for the experimental and control groups
- Give placebo to control group
- Single-blind studies
- Double-blind studies

_____

_____

_____

_____

_____

_____

Generalizing Experimental Conclusions
- Must consider: Would participants have behaved the same way outside of the artificial laboratory situation?
  - Example: Would children in the television study behave the same way at home or school?
- External validity: Do the results generalize to real-world situations?
  - Note: Many "lab" findings do appear to be externally valid

Ethical Principles of Psychological Research: Learning Goals
- Explain the principle of informed consent
- Discuss the roles of debriefing and confidentiality in research
- Discuss the ethical issues involved in animal research

Informed Consent
- Process of gaining permission and providing explanation of:
  - Any risks (physical or emotional) or other factors that might affect decision to participate
  - What procedures are involved
- Participant may stop without penalty
- May not deceive about factors that affect decision to participate

Debriefing and Confidentiality
- Debriefing: After the experimental session is over, telling participant more about the true purpose
  - Explain any deception that took place
- Confidentiality: Researcher does not discuss personal information obtained from the research without permission

Ethics of Animal Research
- Benefits of animal research:
  - Increases experimental control
  - Increased range of possible projects
- Ethical issues in animal research:
  - Informed consent can't be obtained
  - May involve injury or death to the animal
- Ethical guidelines:
  - Care for animals properly
  - Minimize pain and discomfort

Psychology For A Reason: The Tools of Psychological Science
- Observing and describing behavior
  - Naturalistic observation, case studies, and survey research; psychological tests
  - Statistics
- Predicting behavior
–Correlational research
- Explaining behavior
  - Variables; experimental control
- Ethical treatment of humans and animals

Chapter 3: Biological Processes

Chapter 3: Biological Processes

_____

_____

_____

_____

_____

_____

_____

Communicating Internally: Learning Goals
- Communicating internally
- Initiating and coordinating behavior
- Regulating growth and other internal functions
- Adapting and transmitting the genetic code

_____

_____

_____

_____

_____

_____

Communicating Internally: Learning Goals
- Describe the structure, type, and function of neurons
- Explain how neurons transmit information
- Discuss how neurons work together to communicate

_____

_____

_____

_____

_____

_____

Neurons: Types and Functions
- Neurons
  - Sensory
  - Interneurons
  - Motor neurons
- Other cells in the nervous system
  - Glial cells
- Reflexes
  - Example: Pulling away from a hot surface
  - Processed in spinal cord, not brain

Anatomy of a Neuron: Overview
- Dendrites
- Soma
- Axon
- Terminal buttons

Dendrites
- Receive information
- 1000s of branches
  - Enable receiving information from many sources

Soma

- Main "body" of the cell
- Metabolic center
- Genetic material stored here
- Information is processed here

_____

_____

_____

_____

_____

_____

_____

Axon

- Transmits information
- Action potential travels down the axon to other neurons
- Terminal buttons on end
  - These release chemicals

_____

_____

_____

_____

_____

_____

_____

Neural Transmission

- Synapse: Tiny gap between the terminal buttons of one neuron and the dendrite of the next one
- Chemicals flow into the synapse from the terminal buttons
- Neural transmission:
  - Dendrites->Soma->Axon->Terminal Buttons

_____

_____

_____

_____

_____

_____

_____

Resting Potential
- Tiny charge between inside, outside of neuron
- Created by electrically charged particles (ions)
  - Some concentrated outside the cell
- Sodium and chloride ions
  - Some concentrated inside the cell
- Potassium ions
- How is the charge maintained?
  - Sodium-potassium pump
  - Selectively permeable cell membrane

_____

_____

_____

_____

_____

_____

The Action Potential
- Change in potential, primarily because of messages from other neurons
- Excitatory messages:
  - Cell loses the negative charge
- Depolarization
- Inhibitory messages:
  - Cell becomes more negatively charged
- Hyperpolarization

_____

_____

_____

_____

_____

_____

About The Action Potential
- "All or none"
  - Do not vary in strength or intensity
- Travel down the axon between 2 and 200 m.p.h.
- Speed increased if neuron is myelinated
  - Nodes of Ranvier
  - Saltatory conduction

_____

_____

_____

_____

_____

_____

_____

Neurotransmitters

- When action potential reaches the end of the axon, it triggers vesicles (sacs) in the terminal buttons to release chemicals called neurotransmitters
- These activate receptors in the postsynaptic membrane
- May be excitatory or inhibitory, depending on the receptor

Example Neurotransmitters

- Acetylcholine
  - Involved in triggering muscles to contract
- Dopamine
  - Inhibitory effects; dampens and "smooths out" neural messages
- Serotonin
  - Involved in sleep and dreaming
- Gamma-amino-butyric acid (GABA)
  - Involved in regulating anxiety

Drugs and the Brain

- Agonists
  - Mimic the action of neurotransmitters
  - Example: Nicotine mimics acetylcholine
- Antagonists
  - Block the action of neurotransmitters
  - Example: Curare blocks acetylcholine
- Neuromodulators
  - Increase or decrease effectiveness of other neurotransmitters
  - Example: Endorphins

The Communication Network
- Behaviors, thoughts, feelings, arise from pattern of activation across many neurons, not from just one neuron
- Firing rate also communicates information
  - Number of action potentials generated per unit of time
  - Refractory period limits firing rate
- Artificial neural networks can be used to simulate brain's neural systems

_____

_____

_____

_____

_____

_____

Initiating Behavior: Learning Goals
- Describe the basic organization of the nervous system
- Explain the techniques researchers use to study the brain
- Describe the major structures of the brain, and their functions
- Discuss how the two hemispheres coordinate brain functions

_____

_____

_____

_____

_____

_____

_____

Organization of the Nervous System
- Central
  - Brain and spinal cord
- Peripheral
  - Somatic
  - Autonomic
- Sympathetic
  - Prepares body for emergencies
- Parasympathetic
  - Calms the body down

_____

_____

_____

_____

_____

_____

Techniques for Studying the Brain
- Brain damage
  - Case study approach
- Activating the brain electrically or chemically
- Monitoring the brain
  - Electroencephalograph (EEG)
  - Computerized tomography (CT)
  - Positron emission tomography (PET)
  - Magnetic resonance imaging (MRI)

Major Structures of the Brain
- Hindbrain
- Midbrain
- Forebrain

Hindbrain
- Main function: "Life support"
  - Examples: Breathing, heart rate
  - Substructures:
    - Medulla
    - Pons
    - Reticular formation
    - Cerebellum

Midbrain

- Main function: "Relay stations"
  - Coordinates sensory information
- Substructures:
  - Tectum
- Superior colliculus
- Inferior colliculus
  - Substantia nigra

Forebrain

- Main function: "Higher" mental processes
- Substructures:
  - Cerebral cortex
  - Thalamus
  - Hypothalamus
  - Limbic system

Cerebral Cortex

- Left/right hemispheres
- Divided into lobes:
  - Frontal: Planning, decision making, memory, personality
  - Parietal: Processing sensations of touch, temperature, pain
  - Temporal lobes: Auditory processing, speech, language comprehension (left hemisphere)
  - Occipital lobes: Vision

The Case of Phineas Gage
- Illustrates effects of damage to the cerebral cortex
- Railroad construction accident, 1848
- Iron rod driven through skull
  - Frontal lobe damage
- Gage survived
- Personality changes:
  - Unpredictable
  - Crude

The Divided Brain
- In general, left side of cortex handles information from the right side of body/space, and vice versa
- Information does eventually go to both hemispheres
  - Corpus callosum transfers information across hemispheres
- Studies of split-brain patients have told us a great deal about divisions in the brain

Hemispheric Specialization
- Right hemisphere: Spatial tasks, emotions
- Left hemisphere: Verbal tasks
- Is there any such thing as being "left brained" or "right brained?"
  - Not according to well-designed studies
  - Hemispheres normally share information, work together

Regulating Growth and Internal Functions: Learning Goals

- Explain how the endocrine system controls long-term and widespread communication needs
- Discuss the role hormones play in gender-specific behaviors

_____

_____

_____

_____

_____

_____

_____

The Endocrine System

- Communication system that uses the bloodstream rather than neurons
- Hormones
    - Chemicals released by endocrine glands
    - Unlike nervous system, relatively slow, longer-lasting messages
    - Coordinates with nervous system

_____

_____

_____

_____

_____

_____

How the Endocrine System Works

- Hypothalamus controls pituitary gland
- Pituitary controls secretion of hormones from sites in the body
- Examples
    - Testes: Testosterone
    - Ovaries: Estrogen
    - Adrenal glands: Norepinephrine and epinephrine

_____

_____

_____

_____

_____

_____

Are There Gender Effects?

- Hormones determine whether male or female sex organs develop prenatally
- Possible effect on brain development as well
- Some gender effects on task performance
  - Men outperform women on spatial tasks; reverse is true for verbal tasks
- Prenatal hormone exposure has some effect on behavior in childhood
- However: Many gender differences are small

Adapting and Transmitting the Genetic Code: Learning Goals

- Review natural selection and adaptation
- Describe the basic principles of genetic transmission
- Explain how psychologists study genetic influences on behavior

Natural Selection and Adaptations

- Traits are inherited via genes
- Traits can be psychological as well as physical
  - More likely to be passed to offspring if they aid in finding a mate, increase chance of survival
- Natural selection
  - Adaptations: Features selected by nature because they increase odds of survival

Genetic Principles
- Chromosomes: Strips of DNA
  - Half come from mother, half from father
- Genes: Segments of chromosomes that influence particular characteristics
  - Examples: height, hair color
- Dominant genes may mask recessive ones
- Genes may mutate (spontaneously change)

How Genes Translate into Traits
- Phenotype: What you can observe about the trait
  - Example: A person's weight
- Phenotype influenced by:
  - Genotype (genes)
  - Environment
- So: "Final product" usually influenced by heredity AND environment

Studying the Gene-Behavior Link
- Family studies
  - Similarities/differences among blood relatives
  - But: Shared environment may also play a role
- Twin studies
  - Degree of similarity between identical twins vs. fraternal (non-identical) twins

Psychology for a Reason: Biological Solutions
- Communicating Internally
- Initiating and Coordinating Behavior
- Regulating Growth and Internal Functions
- Adapting and Transmitting the Genetic Code

32

Chapter 4: Human Development

Chapter 4: Human Development

_____

_____

_____

_____

_____

_____

_____

What's it For? Developmental Solutions
- Developing Physically
- Developing Intellectually
- Developing Socially and Personally

_____

_____

_____

_____

_____

_____

_____

Developing Physically: Learning Goals
- Describe the physical changes that occur prenatally
- Discuss how we grow from infancy through adolescence
- Discuss adulthood and the aging body and brain

_____

_____

_____

_____

_____

_____

_____

Stages of Prenatal Development
- Germinal period: 0-2 weeks
  - Time from conception to when the zygote implants
- Embryonic period: 2-8 weeks
  - Heartbeat begins; recognizable body parts appear; sexual differentiation begins
- Fetal period: 9th week - birth
  - Last 3 months: Rapid growth of body and brain

_____
_____
_____
_____
_____
_____
_____

Environmental Hazards
- Fetus or embryo affected by:
  - mother's health
  - mother's diet
  - substances such as nicotine, alcohol
  - certain diseases, such as German measles (rubella)
- Teratogens: Environmental agents that can damage the developing child

_____
_____
_____
_____
_____
_____
_____

Effects of Alcohol
- Even moderate drinking (1 drink per day) may cause significant problems
- With heavy drinking: Fetal alcohol syndrome may occur
  - Heavy drinking = 5 or more drinks per day
  - Physical and facial deformities
  - Increased risk of mental retardation

_____
_____
_____
_____
_____
_____
_____

Growth During Infancy

- Weight quadruples in first 2 years
- Brain growth:
  - Reaches 75% of adult size
  - Most growth is in size/complexity of neurons, not addition of new neurons
  - Environment affects brain development
- Motor development
  - Most crawl, stand, and walk at roughly same ages

_____

_____

_____

_____

_____

Growth: Toddlerhood to Adolescence

- Coordination, general processing speed increase throughout childhood
- Puberty (sexual maturity)
  - Girls: Menarche (first menstrual flow) occurs around age 12 or 13
  - Boys: Androgens cause appearance of facial hair, voice change, ability to ejaculate at around age 13 or 14
  - Ability to reproduce usually occurs several months later

_____

_____

_____

_____

_____

The Aging Body

- Strength and agility begin to decline in the twenties
  - Note: There are individual differences
- Reproductive changes: Women
  - Menopause occurs at around age 50
- Ovulation, menstruation stop
- Reproductive changes: Men
  - Some men lose ability to father children, some do not

_____

_____

_____

_____

_____

_____

The Aging Brain
- Neurons do die with age
  - However, they can continue to increase in complexity
- Dementia: Loss in mental functioning caused by physical changes in the brain
  - Fewer than 1% of those over 65 have dementia
  - About 20% over 80 have dementia

_____

_____

_____

_____

_____

Developing Intellectually: Learning Goals
- Explain the research tools used to study infant perception and memory
- Describe an infant's perceptual capabilities
- Characterize memory loss in the elderly
- Discuss and evaluate Piaget's theory of cognitive development
- Discuss and evaluate Kohlberg's theory of moral development

_____

_____

_____

_____

_____

_____

The Tools of Investigation
- Longitudinal design vs. cross-sectional designs
- If you're studying young children:
  - Preference technique
  - Habituation techniques
  - Using rewards

_____

_____

_____

_____

_____

_____

Why These Techniques Work
- Babies generally:
  - prefer some stimuli over others
  - notice new or different things
  - can learn to repeat rewarding activities
- Therefore, researchers can infer what differences babies can detect

_____

_____

_____

_____

_____

_____

Infants' Perceptual Abilities
- Hearing: Can recognize voices within a day or two of birth
- At birth or soon after, infants can:
  - Tell sour, sweet, salty apart
  - Recognize mother's smell
  - Experience pain, soothing touch
- Vision:
  - 2-6 months: Can perceive a dropoff
  - But: Newborn vision blurry, lacks detail

_____

_____

_____

_____

_____

Aging and Memory
- Ability to recall declines, but recognition ability stays nearly the same
- Why?
  - Less able to focus?
  - Influenced by age-related stereotypes?
- Age differences reduced when older adults:
  - Are allowed to use expertise
  - Are given supportive cues, extra time

_____

_____

_____

_____

_____

The Development of Thought: Piaget's Work

- Children think, organize the world meaningfully - but differently than adults
- Schemata: Mental models used to guide and interpret experiences
    - Inaccurate early in childhood
    - Become more adult-like throughout childhood

How Schemata Change

- Assimilation: Fitting experiences into schemata
    - Example: Seeing a horse for the first time and classifying it as a "doggie"
- Accommodation: Changing schemata to accommodate new experiences
    - Example: Creating a new category called "horses"

Piaget's First Stage: The Sensorimotor Period

- Birth to about age 2
- Schemata revolve around babies' sensory, motor abilities
- Early in first year, babies lack object permanence: They fail to realize that objects still exist when out of sight
    - By age 1: Can remember, represent objects symbolically

Piaget's Second Stage: The Preoperational Period

- About ages 2 through 7
- Schemata become more sophisticated
- But: Some errors still persist
  - Difficulty understanding conservation
- Why -> Possibly centration, difficulty understanding reversibility
  - Egocentrism: Seeing world from own perspective only

Piaget's Third Stage: The Concrete Operational Period

- About ages 7 through 11
- Now have the ability to verbalize, visualize, and mentally manipulate objects
  - Understand reversibility, conservation
- Can perform elementary logical tasks (math, problem solving), but…
- Difficulty with true abstract thinking
  - Example: Hypothetical questions

Piaget's Fourth Stage: The Formal Operational Period

- Approximately adolescence (age 11 to adulthood)
- Can consider imaginary concepts, hypothesize, think in the abstract
- Can use systematic ways of solving problems
- Thinking is now adult-like

Was Piaget Right?

- Well-accepted contribution: Children have unique schemata that change systematically over time
- Challenges:
  - Piaget tended to under-estimate children's cognitive abilities, such as object permanence
  - Stages may not be as rigid as he thought
  - Culture affects cognitive development too

Moral Development

- Morality: Ability to tell appropriate from inappropriate actions (or: right from wrong)
- Kohlberg: Modeled a series of moral development stages after Piaget's ideas
- Tested individuals' moral development by posing a moral dilemma:
  - A sick woman's husband cannot afford a drug that will save her life. Should he steal it?

Three Main Levels of Moral Development

- Preconventional: Based on consequences
  - Don't steal - you will be punished
- Conventional: Based on rules, social order
  - Don't steal - stealing is against the law
- Postconventional: Based on abstract principles
  - Don't steal - without the rule of law, society will descend into chaos

Was Kohlberg Right?
- Observational studies confirm some of his ideas
- Challenges:
  - Too much emphasis on an abstract code of justice?
  - Too much emphasis on individualism, instead of on collective goals, not enough on group welfare
- May reflect bias toward Western culture

Developing Socially and Personally: Learning Goals
- Discuss the short- and long-term characteristics of early attachments
- Explain Erik Erikson's stage theory of personal identity development
- Describe the issues that affect gender-role development
- Discuss the psychological issues associated with death and dying

Attachment in Infancy

- Attachments: Strong emotional ties formed to one or more intimate companions
- How does attachment start?
  - Contact comfort: Warm physical contact
  - Harlow's research: Newborn rhesus monkeys become attached to soft objects
- What if a hard wire object gives food, soft one gives nothing? Attach to soft object anyway

Temperament and Early Attachments

- Temperament: General level of emotional reactivity
  - Affects the kinds of comforting responses the baby gets from caregivers
- Strong biological basis
  - Stable across the lifespan
- Temperament types: Easy, difficulty, slow-to-warm-up

Attachment Types

- Gauged with the strange situation test
- Secure: Upset when caregiver leaves, happy when he or she returns
- Resistant: Upset when caregiver leaves, but may seem upset when caregiver returns too
- Avoidant: Not upset when caregiver leaves, little reaction when he or she returns
- Disorganized/disoriented: Inconsistent

What About Child Care?

- Preschoolers in quality day care tend to:
  - Have improved reading and math skills
  - Have better social adjustment
  - Show small or no differences in attachment
- Quality day care means:
  - Safe and clean physical environment
  - Well-trained, positive, cheerful staff
  - Low child-teacher ratio

The Long-Term Effect of Early Attachments

- Some cautions:
  - Attachment quality may vary over time, across caregivers
  - Research findings are correlational
- Later in childhood and on into adulthood friendships are particularly important
  - Strong social networks improve well-being and even health

Personal Identity Development: Erikson's Stage Theory

- Sense of self shaped by psychosocial crises at certain points in life
- Stages in childhood:
  - Infancy: Trust versus mistrust
  - Toddlerhood: Autonomy vs. shame/doubt
  - 3 to 6: Initiative vs. guilt
  - 6 to 12: Industry vs. inferiority
  - Adolescence: Identity vs. role confusion

Erikson's Stages in Adulthood
- Young adulthood: Intimacy vs. isolation
- Middle age: Generativity vs. stagnation
- Old age: Identity vs. despair

_____
_____
_____
_____
_____
_____
_____

Was Erikson Right?
- Well-accepted contributions:
  - Personal development is lifelong
  - Emphasis on social and cultural interactions
- Challenges:
  - Sharp transitions between stages?
  - Mechanisms that allow for resolution?
  - Difficult to test scientifically

_____
_____
_____
_____
_____
_____

Gender-Role Development
- Gender roles: Patterns of behavior consistent with society's dictates
- Gender identity (sense of self as male or female) begins to develop by 2 or 3
  - Children usually do not understand that gender is permanent until elementary age
- Social learning view: Masculine/feminine behavior is mainly learned from environment

_____
_____
_____
_____
_____
_____

Growing Old in Society

- Ageism: Discrimination or prejudice against a person based on age
- Common stereotypes involving the elderly: most are sick, in mental decline, lonely, depressed
  - In fact, older people tend to be more contented, less depressed than younger people
- Some positive stereotypes as well

Death and Dying: Kubler

- Based on interviews with the terminally ill, Kubler-Ross proposed that the typical sequence is denial, anger, bargaining, depression, and acceptance
- Well-accepted contribution: Denial, anger, and depression are normal reactions
- Challenges: Not all dying people go through these stages in this order
  - Alternate idea: Dying trajectories

Psychology for a Reason: The Tools of Development

- Developing Physically
- Developing Intellectually
- Developing Socially and Personally

Chapter 5: Sensation and Perception

Chapter 5: Sensation and Perception

_____

_____

_____

_____

_____

_____

_____

What's it For? Building the World of Experience
- Translating the Message
- Identifying the Message Components
- Producing a Stable Interpretation

_____

_____

_____

_____

_____

_____

_____

Vision: Learning Goals
- Explain how light gets translated into the electrochemical language of the brain
- Discuss how the basic features of the visual message, such as color, are identified by the brain
- Explain how a stable interpretation of visual information is created, and why the interpretation process sometimes produces visual illusions

_____

_____

_____

_____

_____

_____

Translating the Message
- Visible light = One part of the spectrum of all electromagnetic energy
  - Three main properties:
    - Wavelength
    - Intensity
    - Purity
- Enters the eye through the cornea, pupil, and lens

Transduction of Light
- Light strikes the retina, where light-sensitive cells react to light by creating neural impulses
  - Rods: Sensitive to low light
  - Cones: Sensitive to fine detail, color
- Concentrated in the fovea
  - Photopigments chemically react to light
- These break down in bright light, regenerate after time in low light, causing dark adaptation

Processing in the Retina
- Rod and cone cells pass information to bipolar cells, then to ganglion cells
- Ganglion cells have receptive fields, meaning:
  - Input received from a number of other cells
  - Responds only to a particular pattern
- Many have center-surround fields
  - Respond to light in middle, not on periphery, of receptive field

Identifying Message Components

- Neural messages travel to brain via optic nerve
  - Splits at optic chiasm
  - Information from right visual field goes to left hemisphere; info from left visual field goes to right hemisphere
- Next stops: lateral geniculate nucleus and superior colliculus

Identifying Features: The Visual Cortex

- From lateral geniculate nucleus, messages relayed to parts of the occipital lobe that process vision ("visual cortex")
- Visual cortex picks out and identifies components called features
  - Example: Bars of light at a particular angle; corners

Higher-Level Feature Detection

- Some feature detectors respond to more complex patterns, such as corners, moving bars, bars of certain length
- Some respond to faces only
  - In humans, certain forms of brain damage cause prosopagnosia (inability to recognize faces)
- Other parts of the brain specialized to handle other aspects of vision, such as motion

Color Vision: Trichromatic Theory
- Three types of cones in retina, each maximally sensitive to one range of wavelengths
  - Wavelengths correspond to blue, green, and red
- Colors sensed by comparing amount of activation coming from each type
  - Most colors are a mix (such as orange)
- Certain kinds of color blindness result from having wrong kind of photopigment in cones

Color Vision: Opponent Processes
- Trichromatic theory can't explain everything about color vision:
  - Why does yellow seem like a primary color too?
  - Why do we see afterimages of complementary colors?
- Additional process: Receptors in visual system respond positively to one color and negatively to that complementary color

Producing Stable Interpretations
- Perception depends on context, expectations as well as sensory messages
  - Bottom-up processing: Controlled by physical messages delivered to the senses
  - Top-down processing: Controlled by one's beliefs, expectations about the world
- Also: Inborn tendencies to group visual information in certain ways

Laws of Visual Organization: Gestalt Principles

- Proximity: Elements that are close to each other seen as being part of the same object
- Similarity: Items sharing physical properties are put into the same set
- Closure: Figures with gaps or small missing parts of the border are seen as complete
- Good continuation: Lines that are interrupted are seen as continuously flowing
- Common fate: Things moving in the same direction are seen as a group

Object Recognition

- Recognition by components theory (Biederman):
  - Objects broken down into simple geometrical forms (geons) before identifying whole object
  - Easy to identify incomplete or degraded objects this way
- Evidence: Fast, easy recognition of degraded objects as long as geons easily visible

Perceiving Depth: Depth Cues

- Monocular: Require input from only one eye
  - Includes linear perspective, shading, relative size, overlap, and haze
- Binocular: Depend on both eyes
  - Retinal disparity: Difference between location of images in each retina
  - Convergence: How far the eyes turn inward to focus on an object

Motion Perception
- Note: Images always moving around on the retina, whether the objects are still or not!
- Sometimes we perceive motion when there isn't any
  - Phi phenomenon
- A variety of cues contribute to movement perception, including changes in retinal images, relative positions of objects

Perceptual Constancies
- Sensory messages are unstable, always changing, yet we perceive a stable world
  - Size constancy
  - Shape constancy
- How do we do it?
  - Make assumptions that allow us to guess, for example, about relative distances of objects

The Price of Constancy: Perceptual Illusions
- Inappropriate interpretations of physical reality
- Example assumptions, and related illusions:
  - Rooms are rectangular -> Ames room illusion
  - Linear perspective cues -> Ponzo illusion
  - Converging lines are corners -> Müller-Lyer illusion

Cultural Influences on Illusions

- Navajos raised in traditional circular homes (hogans) less subject to Mülller-Lyer illusion
  - Similar findings for traditional Zulu
- However: The illusion still persists to some degree
  - Some inborn tendency toward these illusions, modified by experience

Hearing: Learning Goals

- Explain how sound, the physical message, is translated into the electrochemical language of the brain
- Discuss how pitch information is pulled out of the auditory message
- Explain how the auditory message is interpreted, and how sound is localized

Translating the Message

- Sound is mechanical energy requiring a medium such as air or water to move
  - Caused by vibrating stimulus
  - How fast stimulus vibrates -> Frequency
- What we hear as pitch (high or low)
  - Intensity of the vibration -> Amplitude
- What we experience as loudness
- Measured in decibels (dB)

Entering the Ear

- Outer ear:
  - Sound funnels from pinna toward eardrum
- Middle ear:
  - Malleus, incus, and stapes bones vibrate
- Inner ear:
  - Vibrations sent to cochlea
  - Hair cells on basiliar membrane send signals to brain

Identifying Message Components

- Auditory nerve transmits messages from the hair cells to the auditory cortex
- Place theory: Pitch determined by where hair cells on the basiliar membrane are responding to sound
- Frequency theory: Pitch determined partly by frequency of impulses coming from hair cells
  - High-frequency sounds coded with volleys of firing

Interpreting Sound

- Cells in auditory cortex respond to particular combinations of sounds
- Sounds grouped, organized by pitch
  - Prior knowledge (top-down processing) plays a role as well
- To localize sounds, we compare messages between two ears
  - Time of arrival
  - Intensity

The Skin and Body Senses: Learning Goals

- Explain how sensory messages delivered to the skin (touch and temperature) are translated and interpreted by the brain
- Describe how we perceive and interpret pain
- Discuss the operation and function of the body senses: movement and balance

Skin Senses

- Touch
  - When stimulated by pressure, receptor cells in skin send messages to somatosensory cortex (parietal lobe)
- Temperature
  - Limited knowledge of how it is perceived
  - Cold fibers
  - Warm fibers

The Sense of Pain

- Adaptive reaction by the body to stimuli intense enough to cause tissue damage
- Gate-control theory
  - Impulses from pain receptors can be blocked ("gated") by the spinal cord
- Large fibers: Close the gate
- Small fibers: Open the gate
  - Also: Endorphins

The Body Senses
- Kinesthesia: The ability to sense the position and movement of one's body parts
  - Many systems involved: receptors in muscles, joints and skin; visual feedback
- Vestibular sense: The ability to sense changes in acceleration, posture
  - Inner ear organs that contribute: Semicircular canals, vestibular sacs

The Chemical Senses: Learning Goal
- Describe how chemical stimuli lead to neural activities that are interpreted as different odors and tastes

The Chemical Senses
- Includes smell (olfaction) and taste (gustation)
  - Both involve chemoreceptors
- Smell: Receptor cells in upper part of nasal cavity send messages to olfactory bulb
- Taste: Receptor cells on tongue (taste buds) respond to sweet, bitter, salty, sour tastes
  - Distinct from experience of flavor
  - Relayed to thalamus, somatosensory cortex

Pheromones

- Chemicals that cause highly specific reactions when detected by other members of the species
    - Examples: sexual behavior, aggression
- Do humans react to pheromones, e.g., in perfume?
    - None so far produce reliable reactions

From the Physical to the Psychological: Learning Goals

- Explain stimulus detection, including techniques designed to measure it
- Define difference thresholds, and explain Weber's Law
- Discuss stimulus adaptation and its adaptive value

Stimulus Detection

- Absolute threshold: Intensity level at which people detect the stimulus 50% of the time
    - May vary from trial to trial
- Signal detection technique: Used to determine detection ability; also may vary from trial to trial
    - Compare hits to false alarms, correct rejections to misses

Difference Thresholds and Weber's Law
- Smallest detectable difference in magnitude
  - Just noticeable difference (JND) depends on how intense the stimuli are overall
- Weber's law: Ability to notice a difference in two stimuli is a constant proportion of the size of the standard stimulus
- Sensory adaptation: Tendency of sensory systems to reduce sensitivity to a stimulus source that remains constant

Psychology for a Reason: Building the World of Experience
- Translating the Message
- Identifying Message Components
- Producing Stable Interpretations

Chapter 6: Consciousness

Chapter 6: Consciousness

_____

_____

_____

_____

_____

_____

_____

What's it For? The Value of Consciousness
- Setting Priorities for Mental Functioning
- Sleeping and Dreaming
- Altering Awareness: Psychoactive Drugs
- Altering Awareness: Induced States

_____

_____

_____

_____

_____

_____

Attention: Learning Goals
- Define attention and discuss its adaptive value
- Explain how experiments on dichotic listening can be used to study attention
- Describe automaticity and its effects on awareness
- Describe such disorders as visual neglect and attention deficit/hyperactivity disorder

_____

_____

_____

_____

_____

Attention: Overview
- Internal processes used to set priorities for mental functioning
  - Selective; reflects limitations on how much the brain can process at one time
- Prioritizing is adaptive
  - Make best use of limited cognitive resources
  - Focus on most relevant information

Experiments on Attention: Dichotic Listening
- Technique where different messages are presented simultaneously to each ear
  - Task: Repeat one message, ignore the other
- Unattended message: Little is remembered
  - However, some processing does occur:
- Cocktail party effect
- Treisman's "ear-switching" experiment

Processing without Attention: Automaticity
- Fast and effortless processing that requires little or no focused attention
- When a process is more automatic, the less likely you are to be consciously aware of it
  - Automaticity "frees up" resources for more demanding tasks
- What about subliminal influences?
  - Controlled studies show little or no effect

Disorders of Attention: Visual Neglect
- Tendency to ignore things on one side of the body (usually left)
  - Results from damage to right parietal lobe
  - Symptoms may include: reading only one side of a page, dressing one side of body
- However: Some information from neglected side does get through

Disorders of Attention: Attention Deficit/ Hyperactivity Disorder
- Disorder marked by difficulties in concentrating, sustaining attention for extended periods
  - Sometimes, but not always, associated with hyperactivity
- Some debate about definition, brain areas that are involved, overdiagnosis
  - Treatable with medication and/or training

Sleeping and Dreaming: Learning Goals
- Define biological rhythms and discuss how they are controlled
- Describe the various stages and characteristics of sleep
- Discuss the function and adaptive significance of sleep
- Discuss the function of REM sleep and theories of dreaming
- Describe the various sleep disorders

Biological Rhythms
- Example: regular daily transition from waking to sleep
  - Circadian rhythms: Activities that rise and fall along a 24-hour cycle
- Biological clocks: Structures that control biological rhythms
  - Environment synchronizes these
  - Light is particularly important

_____

_____

_____

_____

_____

_____

_____

Studying Sleep: EEG Recordings
- Short for electroencephalograph
- How they are collected:
  - Electrodes pasted to scalp (painless)
  - Changes in electrical potentials of brain cells recorded in the form of line tracings
- Also called: "Brain waves"
- EEGs reveal regular, cyclic changes in brain activity during sleep

_____

_____

_____

_____

_____

_____

Stages of Sleep
- Stage 1: Theta waves appear
  - Light sleep; person may claim to still be awake
- Stage 2: Sleep spindles, K complexes
  - Person definitely asleep, but may respond to some events, such as noises
- Stage 3 and stage 4: Delta activity
  - Very deep sleep; nonresponsive to most stimuli and slow to awake

_____

_____

_____

_____

_____

REM Sleep

- Begins 70-90 minutes into the sleep cycle
- Changes in physiological pattern including increased heart rate, darting eyes, twitching
- EEG: Resembles waking state
- Dreaming:
  - Most people awakened during REM report dreaming
  - Might dream during some non-REM sleep

The Sleep Cycle

- Cycle through stages, in order, 4-5 times a night
- REM interspersed with other stages
- About 90 minutes per cycle
  - Time in each stage varies
  - REM dominates later stages, especially right before waking

The Function of Sleep

- No one knows exactly why we sleep
- Several hypotheses:
  - Repairing/restoring: "Down time" helps repair normal wear and tear on body and brain
  - Survival value: Stops us from going out when low light puts us at risk for predators

Sleep Deprivation

- In humans: Severe sleep deprivation hurts virtually all aspects of functioning, especially complex tasks
  - Contributes to accidents
- In animals:
  - Internal functions such as temperature can't be regulated; weight loss; immune system and organ failure, even death, may result

The Function of REM and Dreaming

- Lost REM tends to be made up the next night
  - REM rebound
- Traditional view: Wish fulfillment
  - Associated with Freud
  - Way to symbolically act out wishes, desires
- Manifest content versus latent content
  - But: Little evidence for this view, and symbolism can be very subjective

Alternative Views of Dreams

- Activation-synthesis hypothesis: Dreams are the brain's attempt to make sense of random patterns of neural activity
- Explains physiological basis for bizarre dream imagery, but difficult to test
- Other possibilities
  - Problem-solving
  - Practice responses to threats from the environment

Disorders of Sleep: Dyssomnias
- Insomnia: Difficulty initiating or maintaining sleep
  - Many causes
- Hypersomnia: Chronic excessive sleepiness
  - One cause is sleep apnea
- Narcolepsy: Sudden extreme sleepiness
  - Rare

Disorders of Sleep: Parasomnias
- Nightmares: Frightening, anxiety-arousing dreams that occur primarily during REM sleep
  - Cause unknown, but frequent ones may signal a psychological disorder
- Night terrors: Sleeper awakens suddenly in an extreme state of panic
- Sleepwalking: Sleeper rises during sleep and wanders about
- Night terrors and sleepwalking happen during non-REM sleep, tend to go away with age

Psychoactive Drugs: Learning Goals
- Compare neurotransmitters with psychoactive drugs
- Discuss the different categories of psychoactive drugs, with examples of each
- Discuss the psychological factors that influence the effects of psychoactive drugs

Drug Actions and Effects
- Psychoactive drugs: Drugs that affect behavior and mental processes through alterations of conscious awareness
- Work mainly by changing communication channels of neurons
  - May mimic neurotransmitters
- Example: Nicotine
  - May depress or block the action of neurotransmitters
- Example: Some sleeping pills

What can happen with repeated use
- Tolerance: Body adapts to compensate for continued use, such that increasing amounts are needed to produce the same effects
- Drug dependency: Condition in which an individual experiences physical or psychological need for the drug
  - With physical dependency: Withdrawal may result
- Physical reactions when a person stops taking the drug

Categories of Psychoactive Drugs
- Depressants
  - Slow the activity of the central nervous system (CNS)
  - Examples: Ethyl alcohol; barbiturates, tranquilizers
- Stimulants
  - Increase activity of the CNS
  - Examples: Caffeine, nicotine, amphetamines, cocaine, MDMA (Ecstasy)

Categories of Psychoactive Drugs, continued...

- Opiates
  - Depress CNS activity, reduce pain and produce euphoria
  - Examples: opium, heroin, morphine
- Hallucinogens
  - Affect perception, distort idea of reality
  - Examples: LSD, mescaline, psilocybin, marijuana

Psychological Factors

- Same amount of same drug may produce different effects on different people
  - Example: One might feel euphoria, the other one fear
- Factors that can influence the effect:
  - Setting
  - Past experience with the drug
  - User's physical, psychological state

Induced States: Learning Goals

- Describe the physiological and behavioral effects of hypnosis
- Discuss whether hypnosis can be used effectively to enhance memory
- Describe the dissociation and role-playing accounts of hypnosis
- Describe the physical, behavioral, and psychological effects of meditation

The Phenomenon of Hypnosis

- What it is: Any form of social interaction that produces a heightened state of suggestibility in a willing participant
  - Induced by various means
- What it isn't
  - A deep sleep
  - Something that happens only to weak-willed people

_____

_____

_____

_____

_____

_____

Possible Effects of Hypnosis

- Respond to commands in ways that seem automatic, involuntary
  - Can include suggestions to stop certain behaviors such as smoking
- Anesthesia
- What about memory enhancement?
  - Little evidence for this
  - Memories may actually be fabricated

_____

_____

_____

_____

_____

_____

Explaining Hypnosis

- Hypnotic dissociations: Consciousness splits into multiple forms of awareness
- Social role playing: Hypnotized person conforms to what they expect will happen
  - Like acting out a role
  - "Simulated subjects" often produce the same phenomena as hypnotized people

_____

_____

_____

_____

_____

_____

Meditation

- Technique for self-induced manipulation of awareness, often used for the purpose of relaxation and self-awareness
- Goal may include relaxation, focused concentration, clear thoughts
- Can produce physiological changes, such as lowered blood pressure, EEG changes
- Does have some beneficial psychological effects

Psychology for a Reason: Using Consciousness

- Setting Priorities for Mental Functioning
- Sleeping and Dreaming
- Altering Awareness: Psychoactive Drugs
- Altering Awareness: Induced States

Chapter 7: Learning from Experience

Chapter 7: Learning from Experience

_____

_____

_____

_____

_____

_____

_____

What's it For? Learning from Experience
- Noticing and Ignoring
- Learning What Events Signal
- Learning About the Consequences of Our Behavior
- Learning from Others

_____

_____

_____

_____

_____

_____

Noticing and Ignoring: Learning Goal
- Describe and compare habituation and sensitization

_____

_____

_____

_____

_____

Habituation and Sensitization

- Orienting response: Turn toward new event
- After repeated exposure:
  - Habituation: Decline in the tendency to respond to an event that has become familiar through repeated presentation
  - Sensitization: Increased responding to an event that has been repeated

Classical Conditioning: Learning Goals

- Describe the basic elements of classical conditioning
- Discuss why and how conditioned responding develops
- Differentiate among second-order conditioning, stimulus generalization, and stimulus discrimination
- Discuss extinction and conditioned inhibition

Classical Conditioning Overview

- Technique developed to study how simple associations form
- These associations allow us to prepare ourselves for future events
  - Example: Association between flash of lightning and noise of thunder

Pavlov's Discovery
- Pavlov (1849-1936): Russian physiologist
  - Used dogs as research subjects in studies of digestion
- Noticed that salivation often began before food placed in their mouths
  - Pavlov observed that some stimuli produce automatic responses, and other stimuli can start to produce those responses too through a process of learning

The Terminology of Classical Conditioning
- Unconditioned stimulus (US): A stimulus that automatically leads to a response prior to any training
  - Example: Food
- Unconditioned response (UR): The response that is produced automatically, prior to training, on presentation of US
  - Example: Salivation

Terminology of Classical Conditioning, continued...
- Conditioned stimulus (CS): Neutral stimulus that is paired with the US during classical conditioning
  - Example: Feeder's footsteps
- Conditioned response (CR): The learned response produced by the conditioned stimulus
  - Example: Dog salivates (CR) when hearing the feeder's footsteps (CS)

Forming the CS-US Connection
- CS should function as a signal that the US is about to occur
- Such a signal is most effective when it:
  - Comes before the US, not after it or at the same time
  - The US follows it closely in time
- Long delay -> Learning less likely
  - Provides new information about the US
- Other stimuli may create "blocking"

Why Does Conditioned Responding Develop?
- The CS doesn't just "substitute" for the US
- CR isn't always the same as the UR
  - Example: Rats "freezing" instead of jumping when a shock is about to occur
  - Cognitive view of classical conditioning
- Second-order conditioning: Procedure in which an established CS is used to condition a second neutral stimulus

Stimulus Generalization
- Responding to a new stimulus in a way similar to the response to an established CS
  - Similar stimulus -> Similar CR
  - Famous example created by J. Watson
- •"Little Albert" conditioned to fear white rats; fear extended to rabbits, fur coats
- Stimulus discrimination: Responding differently to a new stimulus than one responds to an established CS

Extinction: When the CS No Longer Signals the US

- Extinction: Presenting a CS repeatedly, after conditioning, without the US, resulting in a loss in responding
  - Example: Food no longer follows a bell, so dog gradually stops salivating in response to the bell
- Spontaneous recovery: Recovery of an extinguished CR after a period of nonexposure to the CS

Conditioned Inhibition: Signaling the Absence of the US

- Learning that an event signals the absence of the US
  - Example: Bell + light = No food
- Won't drool when the light is presented
- Might produce a response opposite of original CR, such as leaving food area
- Conditioned inhibitors can serve as "safety signals" when US is something dangerous

Operant Conditioning: Learning Goals

- Define operant conditioning and discuss the law of effect
- Explain what we mean by the discriminative stimulus
- Define reinforcement and punishment and distinguish between their positive and negative forms
- Discuss and compare the different schedules of reinforcement

Operant Conditioning Learning Goals, continued...

- Explain how complex behaviors can be acquired through shaping
- Discuss how biological factors might limit the responses that can be learned

Learning about Consequences: Operant Conditioning

- Procedure for studying how organisms learn about the consequences of their own voluntary actions
    - Example: Learning that studying leads to a good exam grade
- Law of effect (Thorndike)
    - If a response is followed by a satisfying consequence, it will be strengthened; if followed by an unsatisfying consequence, it will be weakened

The Discriminative Stimulus: Knowing When to Respond

- Discriminative stimulus: Stimulus situation in which a response will be followed by reward or punishment
    - Can be a particular situation or thing in the environment
- May produce the behavior in response to a similar stimulus (stimulus generalization), unless it doesn't produce same reward (stimulus discrimination)

Reinforcement
- Response consequences that increase likelihood of responding in a similar way again
- Positive reinforcement: Event that, when presented after a response, increases likelihood of that response occurring again
- Negative reinforcement: Event that, when removed after a response, increases likelihood of that response occurring again

Positive Reinforcement
- Usually involves an appetitive stimulus - something the organism needs, likes, wants
  - However, what matters in defining it as positive is the effect on behavior, not subjective qualities
- Response deprivation: Event is reinforcing if it allows you to engage in something that you're deprived of
  - Example: Eating when you are very hungry

Negative Reinforcement
- Response leads to removal of some stimulus
  - Example: Shutting off a loud alarm clock
- Escape conditioning: Response ends the stimulus
  - Example: Animal escaping ongoing shock
- Avoidance conditioning: Response prevents the stimulus
  - Example: Animal escaping before shock

Punishment

- Consequences that decrease the likelihood of responding in a similar way again
- Positive punishment: Presentation of an event after responding lowers likelihood of that response
  - Example: Scolding
- Negative punishment: Removal of an event after responding lowers likelihood
  - Example: Taking away allowance

Punishment: Practical Considerations

- Does effectively suppress behavior
  - Example: A child fighting with a sibling
- Limitation: Does not promote better, alternative behavior
  - Example: Does not teach a child to cooperate with sibling
  - Better: Reinforce an alternative response
- May also increase aggression

Schedules of Reinforcement

- Rule that an experimenter uses to determine when particular responses will be reinforced
- Continuous: Every response followed rapidly by reinforcement
  - Example: Salesperson paid for each sale
- Partial: Reinforcement delivered only some of the time
  - Ratio
  - Interval

Fixed-Ratio Schedules
- Number of responses required for reinforcement doesn't change
  - Example: Salesperson paid for every 10 sales
- Tend to produce steady, consistent rates of responding, but might stop for a period after reinforcement
- Extinction when reinforcement no longer given

Variable-Ratio Schedules
- A certain number of responses required for reinforcement, but this number changes
  - Example: Salesperson paid after some number of sales, but doesn't know how many
- Extinction takes much longer

Interval Schedules
- Fixed-interval: Reinforcement delivered for first response after a fixed interval of time
  - Example: Salesperson paid for first sale in each week, but none until next week
  - Tend to produce low rates of responding
- "Scalloping" pattern
- Variable-interval: Time until reinforcement changes
  - Example: Salesperson paid for first sale on a randomly chosen day

Acquiring Complex Behaviors: Shaping
- Problem: Complex behaviors unlikely to occur spontaneously, so they are hard to reinforce
- Solution: Shaping
  - A procedure in which reinforcement is delivered for successive approximations of the desired response
  - Or: Demanding behaviors closer to the desired one before reward is given

Biological Constraints on Learning
- With enough time and reinforcers, is it possible to teach just any response?
- Genetic constraints influence what can be learned
  - Example: Animals have innate tendencies that limit what they can be trained to do
  - Humans also have innate tendencies to learn certain things more easily
- Example: Fear of snakes

Observational Learning: Learning Goals
- Describe observational learning and the conditions that lead to effective modeling
- Explain why observational learning is adaptive and discuss its practical effects

Observational Learning: Overview
- Learning that occurs as a result of observing the experiences of others
- Consider: What would life be like if you could only learn through your own trial and error?
  - Adaptive to learn from others
- Observational learning occurs in many species, including chimpanzees, rhesus monkeys and some birds

Modeling
- Natural tendency to imitate behavior of significant others
- Strongest when:
  - Model is viewed positively
  - Model is rewarded for the behavior
- Bandura: Showed kids a film of an adult hitting a "Bobo" doll
  - Kids imitated behavior, especially when the adult was praised for the aggression

Observational Learning: Practical Considerations
- Particularly relevant to children
- Modeling techniques such as films have been used to reduce fears, promote positive behavior
- However, television may produce modeling of negative behaviors
  - Aggression
  - Gender stereotyping
  - Unrealistic beliefs about society

Psychology for a Reason: The Value of Learning from Experience

- Learning About Events
- Learning About the Consequences of Behavior
- Learning from Others

_____

_____

_____

_____

_____

_____

_____

Chapter 8: Memory

Chapter 8: Memory

_____

_____

_____

_____

_____

_____

_____

_____

What's it For? Remembering and Forgetting
- Remembering Over the Short Term
- Storing Information for the Long Term
- Recovering Information with Cues
- Updating Memory

_____

_____

_____

_____

_____

_____

_____

Memory: Overview
- Memory: The capacity to preserve and recover information
- Involves several important processes:
  - Encoding: How memories are formed
  - Storage: How memories are kept over time
  - Retrieval: How memories are recovered and translated into performance

_____

_____

_____

_____

_____

_____

Remembering over the Short Term: Learning Goals

- Discuss how visual and auditory sensory memories can be measured
- Describe how information is represented, maintained, and forgotten over the short term

Sensory Memory

- Exact replica of an environmental message which usually lasts for a second or less
    - Iconic memory (vision)
    - Echoic memory (audition)
- Sperling's procedure for measuring it: Show visual array very briefly, ask for partial report (just one row)
    - Partial report much better than full report
- Efron's observation: Sounds seem to linger

Short-Term Memory

- A system we use to temporarily store, think about, reason with information
- The "inner voice"
    - We tend to recode (translate) information into inner speech
- The "inner eye"
    - We can also code information visually, using images

Evidence for the inner voice and inner eye

- Inner voice:
  - Mistakes made during short-term recall tend to sound like, but not look like, the correct items
- Example: Might mistake "B" for "V"
- Inner eye:
  - Judgments made based on mental images are similar to those based on actual pictures

_____

_____

_____

_____

_____

_____

Short-Term Forgetting

- Can prolong short-term memories indefinitely through rehearsal (internal repetition)
- Without rehearsal, memories disappear after 1-2 seconds

_____

_____

_____

_____

_____

_____

_____

What's the capacity of short-term memory?

- Memory span: Number of items that can be recalled from short-term memory, in order, on half of the tested memory trials
  - It's about 7 plus or minus 2 items
- Not absolute; also depends on:
  - How quickly items can be rehearsed
  - Chunking
- Rearranging incoming information into meaningful or familiar patterns

_____

_____

_____

_____

_____

_____

_____

The Working Memory Model

- Several distinct mechanisms:
  - Phonological loop: Like the inner voice; stores word sounds
  - Visuospatial sketchpad: Stores visual and spatial information
  - Central executive: Determines which mechanism to use, coordinates among them
- Brain damage can selectively affect a single mechanism

Storing Information for the Long Term: Learning Goals

- Define episodic, semantic, and procedural memories
- Explain why it's important to form an elaborate and distinctive memory record
- Describe some simple mnemonic techniques

What's Stored in Long-Term Memory?

- Episodic memory: Memory of a particular event or episode that happened to you personally
- Semantic memory: Knowledge about the world, stored as facts that make little/no reference to one's personal experiences
- Procedural memory: Knowledge about how to do things
  - Includes athletic skills, everyday skills such as bike riding, shoe tying

Elaboration

- An encoding process that involves forming connections between to-be-remembered input and other information in memory
  - Helps you retrieve the information later
- Ways to promote elaboration:
  - Think about meaning
  - Notice relationships
  - Notice differences
- Tends to produce distinctive memories, which are easier to retrieve

Flashbulb Memories

- Rich records of the circumstances surrounding emotionally significant and surprising events
- Example events that could produce flashbulb memories: Kennedy assassination, *Challenger* disaster, attacks of 9/11/01
- Surprisingly, these can be inaccurate
  - We tend to incorporate later experiences into our memories

Other Ways to Achieve Elaboration

- Form mental pictures
  - Forces you to think about details
- Space repetitions
  - Distributed practice: Practice material at intervals; do something else in between
- Consider sequence position
  - Memory for items in a list is best for those at the beginning (primacy) and end (recency)

Mnemonic Techniques
- Mental tricks that help people think about material in ways that improve memory
  - Most depend on visual imagery
- Method of loci: Choose a familiar pathway, then form visual images of to-be-remembered items sitting along the pathway
- Peg-word method: Form visual images connecting to-be-remembered items with retrieval cues ("pegs")
  - Variation: Linkword method
- Link sound to meaning, imagery

_____
_____
_____
_____
_____
_____
_____

Recovering Information from Cues: Learning Goals
- Discuss the importance of retrieval cues in remembering
- Explain the role of schemas in reconstructive memory
- Discuss the differences between explicit and implicit memory

_____
_____
_____
_____
_____
_____

The Importance of Retrieval Cues
- Compare these testing conditions:
  - Free recall: Remember information without explicit retrieval cues
  - Cued recall: Remember based on a cue
- Cued recall produces substantially better performance
- Conclusion: Cues play a critical role in recall

_____
_____
_____
_____
_____
_____
_____

How Cues Work

- Encoding-retrieval match: Better memory when cue matches the memory that was encoded
- Transfer-appropriate processing: Using the same kinds of mental processes during study and testing improves memory
  - Using same processes ensures that during study, you will attend to the cues that will be present when you try to recall

_____

_____

_____

_____

_____

_____

Reconstructive Remembering:

- We tend to "fill in" parts of our memories based on past experience, expectations
- Schemas: Organized knowledge structure in long-term memory
  - Or: Clusters of related facts
  - We sometimes distort memories to fit schemas
- Famous example: "The War of the Ghosts" (Bartlett)

_____

_____

_____

_____

_____

_____

Other Research on Reconstruction

- Loftus and Palmer (1974): Speed estimates for a witnessed car crash are affected by wording of the question
  - Example: "Smashed" versus "contacted"
- False memory paradigm
  - Example: *bed rest awake tired dream...* leads to falsely remembering *sleep*
- Reconstruction is probably adaptive, but can result in memory errors

_____

_____

_____

_____

_____

_____

Remembering Without Awareness: Implicit Memory

- Remembering that occurs in the absence of conscious awareness or willful intent
  - Contrast to explicit memory: Conscious, willful remembering
  - Example implicit memory test: Completing a fragment of a word or picture
- Encoding-retrieval match matters here too
  - But: Elaboration has a much reduced effect on implicit memory

Updating Memory: Learning Goals

- Discuss the contributions of Ebbinghaus and explain why forgetting is often adaptive
- Describe the mechanisms that cause forgetting, including decay and retroactive and proactive interference
- Discuss motivated forgetting, and the case for repression
- Describe retrograde and anterograde amnesia, and explain where memories might be stored in the brain

How Quickly Do We Forget?

- Depends on:
  - How it was initially encoded
  - Whether it was encountered again later
  - Kinds of retrieval cues present at time of remembering
- Ebbinghaus' work: Documented the forgetting function
  - Rapid loss, followed by gradual decline
  - Based on memory for nonsense syllables

Why Is Forgetting Adaptive?

- Must update memory, discriminate one occurrence from another
  - Example: Where you parked your car today, not yesterday
- Case of "S.," who could not forget (Luria)

Why Do We Forget?

- Decay: Idea that memories fade with time
  - However: This can't explain why "forgotten" memories can be retrieved with the right cues
- More plausible: Interference
  - Retroactive interference: Formation of new memories hurts retention of old memories
  - Proactive interference: Old memories interfere with the establishment and recovery of new memories

Motivated Forgetting

- Refers to times when it's better to forget, or when we consciously try to do so
- The evidence for repression:
  - We do tend to recall more pleasant than unpleasant things
  - Some people report not being able to recall sexual abuse, and documented sexual abuse is not always recalled in adulthood
- However, we may simply rehearse pleasant events more, not actively repress bad ones

The Neuroscience of Forgetting
- Amnesia: Forgetting caused by physical problems in the brain
- Retrograde amnesia affects events that happened prior to the point of injury
  - Often a temporary result of injury
- Anterograde amnesia affects events that happened after the point of injury
  - Tends to be permanent
  - However, implicit memory may be spared

Psychology for a Reason: Remembering and Forgetting
- Remembering Over the Short Term
- Storing Information for the Long Term
- Recovering Information with Cues
- Updating Memory

Chapter 9: Language and Thought

Chapter 9: Language and Thought

_____

_____

_____

_____

_____

_____

_____

What's it For? Cognitive Processes
- Communicating with Others
- Classifying and Categorizing
- Solving Problems
- Making Decisions

_____

_____

_____

_____

_____

_____

Communicating with Others: Learning Goals
- Understanding the structure of language
- Isolating the factors that contribute to language comprehension
- Identifying the major milestones of language development
- Assessing language in nonhuman species
- Evaluating the possibility that language is an adaptation

_____

_____

_____

_____

_____

The Structure of Language
- Grammar sets language apart from other communication systems
  - Set of rules that allow the communicator to combine arbitrary symbols to convey meaning
  - Three aspects:
- Phonology: Rules for word sounds
- Syntax: Rules for combining words
- Semantics: Rules used to communicate meaning

The Hierarchical Structure of Language
- Phonemes: Smallest significant sound units in speech
  - Example: "ee" as in "feet"
- Morphemes: Smallest units of language that carry meaning
  - Examples: "do," "un"
- Words, phrases, and sentences
  - Words combine to make phrases
- Example: "the interesting class" is a noun phrase

The Structure of Sentences
- Rules of syntax determine how words combine into phrases, and phrases into sentences
- Chomsky's idea of how sentences work:
  - Surface structure: Superficial appearance, literal ordering of words
  - Deep structure: Underlying representation of meaning
  - Producing sentences requires transformation of deep structure into a surface structure

Language Comprehension

- How do we decide what another person is trying to communicate?
  - Communication depends on common knowledge among speakers
- Pragmatic rules: How practical knowledge is used to comprehend speaker's intention, produce an effective response
  - Example pragmatic guidelines (Grice): Be informative, tell the truth, be relevant, be clear

Language Development

- Is language a product of genes or experience?
  - Babies follow similar milestones all over the world
- Babies are born producing phonemes appropriate for many languages, but soon narrow these down
  - By 3-5 weeks: Cooing
  - By 4-6 months: Babbling
  - By 6-18 months: More like adult speech

Child Speak

- By the end of the third year, telegraphic speech begins
  - Simple two-word sentences
  - Word order almost always correct
- Sophisticated grammar skills learned during the preschool years, with little formal teaching
  - Preschoolers tend to overgeneralize rules
- Example: *goed, foots*
- Grammatical knowledge fine-tuned from 3 to about 6 or 7

Language in Nonhuman Species

- Nonhuman animals definitely communicate, but not all communication is language
- Attempts to teach chimps to speak failed
- Signs/symbol communication in chimps:
  - Chimps such as Washoe, Sarah, and Kanzi have learned to use these
- Is it really language?
  - Can they generate new combinations?
  - Can they learn from other chimps?
  - Psychologists disagree on the answer

Is Language an Adaptation?

- Many scientists believe that natural selection caused this special ability to develop
  - Survival advantage
- Evidence for adaptation view includes special brain regions for language, specially developed vocal tract, similarity of languages all around the world
  - However: Fossil record can't show how or when it developed, or why

Classifying and Categorizing: Learning Goals

- Understanding how categories and category membership are defined
- Distinguishing between prototype and exemplar views of categorization
- Explaining the hierarchical organization of categories

Classifying and Categorizing

- Category: Class of objects that most people agree belong together
  - Being able to categorize is adaptive
- Important questions about categorizing:
  - What properties about an object make it belong to a particular category?
  - Do we form abstract category representations?
  - Are categories organized into hierarchies?

Defining Category Membership

- Example: You know that Monopoly is an example of the category "game," but why?
- Defining features view: Categories are defined by features that all members share
  - But: Many categories don't have features shared by all; boundaries are fuzzy
- Family resemblance view: Members of a category share certain core features, but not all members have to have all these features

Do People Store Category Prototypes?

- Prototype: Best or most representative member of a category
  - Could categorize by storing prototypes, comparing exemplars (examples) to them.
- Alternative: Store all examples of the category
- Could categorize by comparing each exemplar to all the other ones
- Different researchers disagree on this question; perhaps we do both

The Hierarchical Structure of Categories

- Most objects can be categorized in several ways
    - Example: Monopoly -> "board game," "game," "activity"
    - How do we organize different categories?
- Basic-level category: Used most often, is most useful and predictive
- Superordinate categories: More general, less descriptive
- Subordinate-level categories: Very specific

Solving Problems: Learning Goals

- Distinguishing between well- and ill-defined problems
- Describing the pitfalls of problem representation
- Comparing algorithms and heuristics
- Describing the Aha! moment in problem solving

Problem Types

- Well-defined: Goal and starting point are clear; you know when it's been solved
    - Example: Algebra problems
- Ill-defined: Goal and starting point are unclear; hard to tell when solution is reached
    - Many real-life problems are ill-defined
    - Example: What is the secret to having a happy life?

Representing Problem Information
- To solve a problem, you need to understand what information is given and how that information can potentially be used
- Functional fixedness: Tendency to see objects and their functions in fixed and typical ways
    - Failure to restructure the way you think about elements in the problem

Developing Strategies
- Two kinds of strategies:
    - Algorithms: Step-by step procedures that guarantee a solution
    - Heuristics: "Shortcuts" that are efficient, but don't guarantee a solution
- Need to avoid "mental set": Tendency to rely on problem-solving strategies that were successful in the past

Common Heuristics
- Means-end analysis
    - Find actions (means) that reduce the gap between the current starting point and goal (ends)
    - Usually requires breaking down problem into subgoals
- Working backward
- Searching for analogies

The Aha! Moment
- Insight: Process by which solution seems to "magically" pop into mind
  - Tends to be sudden, rather than systematic progression toward solution
- What causes it to happen?
  - Difficulty of re-creating and studying insight in laboratory studies makes this difficult to answer
  - Answer is largely a mystery

Making Decisions: Learning Goals
- Understanding how "framing" alternatives influences decision making
- Identifying common decision-making biases
- Describing the common decision-making heuristics
- Evaluating the pros and cons of using heuristics

The Framing of Decision Alternatives
- Framing: How alternatives are presented
  - Example: Is a course of action framed as a way to ensure a gain, or avoid a loss?
  - People tend to avoid risks when gain is emphasized, take risks when loss is emphasized
- Framing can lead to irrational choices
  - Example: Doctors are more likely to choose a treatment they see as preventing death, as opposed to extending life

Decision-Making Biases
- Confirmation bias: Tendency to seek out and use information that supports and confirms a prior decision or belief
  - People avoid seeking out information that might contradict a prior belief
- Belief persistence: Tendency to cling to initial beliefs even when confronted with disconfirming evidence
  - People tend to try to find reasons why beliefs could still be true, even with contradictory evidence

Representativeness
- When judging likelihood of something falling into a class, compare the similarity of that thing to the average member of that class
- Example: Which is probably a random series of coin flips, H H H T T T or H T T H T H?
  - Both are equally likely, but one is more representative
- Mistakes that can result from representativeness:
  - Ignoring the base rate
  - Conjunction error

Availability
- Base estimates on odds of an event occurring on ease with which examples of the effect come to mind
- Example: Diseases that get a lot of publicity are estimated to be more common than other diseases
- Example: You believe it's more likely that you will do the dishes than your roommate
  - You remember all the times you did the dishes, but not as many times your roommate did them

Anchoring-and-Adjustment
- Judgments are influenced by starting points, such as initial estimates
- Example: What percent of African countries belong to the United Nations?
  - "More than or less than 65?" -> Higher estimate
  - "More than or less than 10%" -> Lower estimate

_____

_____

_____

_____

_____

_____

Heuristics: Pros and Cons
- Research on heuristics emphasizes the serious mistakes we make
- Good things about heuristics:
  - In real life, we often make good decisions anyway
  - They are faster and easier to use than optimal reasoning strategies
  - Oftentimes, we don't have the statistical information for optimal reasoning anyway

_____

_____

_____

_____

_____

_____

Psychology for a Reason: Cognitive Processes
- Communicating with Others
- Classifying and Categorizing
- Solving Problems
- Making Decisions

_____

_____

_____

_____

_____

_____

Chapter 10: Intelligence

Chapter 10: Intelligence

_____

_____

_____

_____

_____

_____

_____

What's it For? The Study of Intelligence
- Conceptualizing Intelligence
- Measuring Individual Differences
- Discovering the Sources of Intelligence

_____

_____

_____

_____

_____

_____

_____

Conceptualizing Intelligence: Learning Goals
- Understanding the psychometric approach to intelligence, including Spearman's two-factor theory
- Distinguishing between fluid and crystallized intelligence
- Explaining how the speed of neural transmission might influence intelligence
- Evaluating the various theories of multiple intelligences

_____

_____

_____

_____

_____

_____

What Is Intelligence?
- Adaptive mind perspective: Ability to solve the problems that are unique to your environment
  - Advantage of this perspective: Isn't just unique to humans
- However, individual differences need to be considered as well

Psychometrics: Measuring the Mind
- Psychometric view: Intelligence is a mental capacity that can be understood by analyzing performance on mental tests
- First attempts at psychometrics carried out by Galton (1822-1911)
  - Conducted batteries of sensory, physical, intellectual tests
  - However: Scores were poor predictors of real-world performance

Spearman's Work in Psychometrics
- Developed factor analysis
  - A procedure that groups together related items on tests by analyzing correlations
- Scores that reflect a single underlying ability should correlate
- Argued that a single factor, g, underlies performance on a variety of mental tests
- But: A separate factor, s (for specific intelligence), is unique to each particular test
  - Two-factor theory: g and s

Hierarchical Models

- Some argue for several kinds of primary mental ability instead of just one *g*–Examples include verbal comprehension, verbal fluency, numerical ability, spatial ability, memory, perceptual speed, reasoning
- Hierarchical idea: *G* exists, but is made up of subfactors (abilities) that may operate independently from one another

Fluid and Crystallized Intelligence

- Many researchers accept the idea of general intelligence, but divide it into two components
- Fluid intelligence: Ability to solve problems, reason, and remember
  - Relatively uninfluenced by experience, schooling
- Crystallized intelligence: Knowledge and abilities acquired as a result of experience
  - Reflects schooling, cultural background

Speed of Neural Transmission

- Individual differences in the speed with which neurons communicate might help explain individual differences in intelligence
- Evidence for this view:
  - Electrical response of the brain to a visual stimulus (P100) correlates with intelligence test scores
- However: This research was only correlational, and could not explain all of the variability in intelligence test scores

Multiple Intelligences: Gardner's Case Study Approach

- People sometimes show specialized skills or abilities that are not representative of a general ability
  - A person can have great skills in one area, but deficits in another area
- Gardner's view: An *intelligence* is an ability that permits problem solving or making products in one particular area
  - Study this by looking at individuals with special abilities or talents

Gardner's Multiple Intelligences

- Musical
- Bodily-kinesthetic
- Logical-mathematical
- Linguistic
- Spatial
- Interpersonal
- Intrapersonal
- Naturalist

Multiple Intelligences: Sternberg's Triarchic Theory

- Combines Gardner's broad conception of intelligence with a concern for the mental operations that underlie each part of intelligence
- Three parts:
  - Analytic intelligence
  - Creative intelligence
  - Practical intelligence

Measuring Individual Differences: Learning Goals

- Understanding the components of a good test
- Understanding and evaluating IQ
- Defining mental retardation and giftedness
- Assessing the validity of IQ tests and the effects of labeling
- Contrasting creativity, emotional intelligence, and tacit knowledge

"Good" Intelligence Tests Have:

- Reliability
  - Reliable tests produce similar results with repeated administration to the same person
- Standardization: Practice of keeping the testing, scoring, and interpretation procedures consistent across all administrations of a test
  - Well-standardized tests are administered the same way to every test taker, every time

Another characteristic of good tests: Validity

- How well a test measures what it is supposed to measure
- Content validity: Does it sample broadly from the domain of interest?
- Predictive validity: Does it predict a future outcome, such as job or school success?
- Construct validity: How well a test applies to a particular theoretical construct
  - Example: Theoretical idea of "creativity"

IQ: The Intelligence Quotient

- Invented in 1904 by French psychologists Binet and Simon
    - Purpose: Identify students with special educational needs
- Mental age: Chronological age that best fits a child's level of performance, calculated by comparing with average test scores from different age groups
    - Intelligence quotient: [Mental age / Chronological age] * 100

Another approach: Deviation IQ

- An intelligence score derived from determining where your performance sits in an age-based distribution of test scores
    - Average score for a particular age group = 100; score determined by how much more or less you scored relative to others in your age group
- Helps overcome problem of comparing scores across age groups

Extremes of Intelligence: Mental Retardation

- Definition: Scoring below 70 on a standard IQ test
- Affects between 1% and 3% of population
    - Many are able to live independently
- Many causes, including:
    - Genetic abnormalities
    - Environmental factors
    - Teratogens

Giftedness

- Definition: Scoring above 130 on a standard IQ test
- Do gifted children grow up to be successful, socially well adjusted, and happy?
  - Some research suggests yes (Terman)
  - Profoundly gifted children do seem to show some emotional, social problems as adults (Winner)
- A special case: Savants, who have amazing abilities in only limited domains
  - Associated with disorders such as autism

How Valid Is IQ?

- Different specific IQ tests: WAIS, WISC, Stanford-Binet
- These tend to correlate well with school performance, but not as well with broader measures of how a person adapts to environment
- Labeling effects: Does being labeled as high-IQ or low-IQ tend to affect educational opportunities?
  - If so, IQ can become a self-fulfilling prophecy

Individual Differences Related to Intelligence

- Creativity: Ability to generate ideas that are original, novel, useful
  - Not well correlated to IQ
- Emotional intelligence: Ability to perceive, understand, express emotion in useful, adaptive ways
  - Little is known about it
- Tacit knowledge: Unspoken practical knowledge about how to perform a job well
  - Usually not assessed by IQ tests

Discovering the Sources of Intelligence: Learning Goals

- Understanding how IQ changes with age
- Explaining how twin studies are used to evaluate genetic contributions to intelligence
- Understanding environmental influences on intelligence, and how they interact with genetic influences

The Stability of IQ

- Results of longitudinal studies suggest IQ is fairly stable until about age 60
  - Studied longitudinally, meaning studying the same people repeatedly as they age
- After age 60, no drastic loss in IQ
- Crystallized intelligence declines less than fluid intelligence
  - May reflect loss of neural transmission speed, but addition of new knowledge

Stability of IQ in Populations: The Flynn Effect

- IQ test performance in general seems to be rising over time
  - Decade-by-decade increases observed since 1930s
- Explanations for the Flynn effect?
  - Better nutrition?
  - Exposure to new technologies?
  - Exposure to preschool or daycare?
- True cause remains a mystery

Genetic Influences on Intelligence: Twin Studies

- Compare IQ scores of twins separated through adoption
  - Fraternal twins: Different genetics
  - Identical twins: Identical genetics
- Tend to have more similar IQs than fraternal twins
- Heritability: Mathematical index of the extent to which IQ differences can be accounted for by genetic factors
  - Many researchers propose 70% heritability for intelligence

The Case for Environmental Influences on Intelligence

- Many researchers agree on some degree of heritability, but not 100%
  - Therefore, environment has some role
- Controversial issue: What accounts for ethnic group differences in IQ scores?
  - Probably not genetics
  - Other sources: Economic differences, test bias, cultural experiences that lead to good test performance

Other Factors that May Cause Between-Group IQ Differences

- Test bias
  - Most traditional IQ tests written, administered, and scored by white, middle-class psychologists
  - Terms, expressions, knowledge tested might be unfamiliar to some individuals
- Stereotype threat: People's expectations affect how they score
  - Example: African Americans may expect to do poorly on intelligence tests

How "Nature" and "Nurture" Might Interact

- Recall from chapter 3: Genotype versus phenotype
  - Environment affects how genes are expressed
- Example: Environment and genes determine how tall a particular plant will grow
- "Two-way street" between genes and experience
  - Having certain genes also affects the experiences you will have

Psychology for a Reason: The Study of Intelligence

- Conceptualizing Intelligence
- Measuring Individual Differences
- Discovering the Sources of Intelligence

Chapter 11: Motivation and Emotion

Chapter 11: Motivation and Emotion

_____

_____

_____

_____

_____

_____

_____

What's It For? Motivation and Emotion
- Activating Behavior
- Meeting Biological Needs
  - Hunger and Eating
  - Sexual Behavior
- Expressing and Experiencing Emotion

_____

_____

_____

_____

_____

_____

_____

Activating Behavior: Learning Goals
- Compare instinct and drive and their roles in activating behavior
- Understand incentive motivation and its role in activating behavior
- Compare achievement motivation and intrinsic motivation
- Describe Maslow's hierarchy of needs

_____

_____

_____

_____

_____

_____

Instincts

- Unlearned characteristic patterns of responding controlled by specific triggering stimuli in the world
  - Examples: Birds build nests, cats hunt
- Important in animal behavior, but in humans?
  - How many human instincts are there?
  - How do we define them?
- Out of favor as an explanation for human behavior

Drives

- Psychological states that arise in response to internal physiological needs
  - Examples: Hunger, thirst
- Homeostasis: Process through which body maintains a steady state
  - Example: Important to maintain a constant internal temperature
  - Reducing drive -> Restore homeostasis
- More flexible concept than instinct

Incentive Motivation

- External factors in the environment that exert "pulling" effects on our actions
  - Example: Good grades motivate you to study
- Interact with internal factors
  - An internal drive, such as hunger, can increase motivating effect of an incentive, such as a food reward

Achievement Motivation

- Internal drive or need for achievement, possessed by all individuals to varying degrees
  - Reflected by how much a person values, needs individual achievement
- Affected by past experience
  - Example: Effect of praise on children
- Some cultures value individual achievement more than others

Intrinsic Motivation

- Goal-directed behavior that seems to be entirely self-motivated
  - Actions that are rewarding for their own sake
- Can actually be reduced by external rewards
  - Example: Rewarding children for drawing makes drawing less intrinsically rewarding

Maslow's Hierarchy of Needs

- Needs differ in origin: some biological, some psychological
  - Which ones come first?
- Maslow: Needs are prioritized
  - Physiological come first; others such as social and esthetic needs come later
- Unfilled needs lead to action
  - Difficult to test scientifically, but influential

Hunger and Eating: Learning Goals
- Understand how internal and external factors influence the desire to eat
- Explain how body weight is regulated
- Distinguish between anorexia nervosa and bulimia nervosa

Internal Factors
- Brain monitors signals from the body
  - Glucose (sugar)
  - Insulin (hormone released by pancreas)
- Hypothalamus especially important for regulating hunger
  - Lesioning drastically affects eating and weight
- Other important regions: brain stem, hippocampus

External Factors
- Eating habits involving times, places, kinds of food you're used to can affect food choices
  - Includes cultural differences in eating customs
- Food cues can trigger eating as well, even when a person does not physically need food
  - Includes sight, smell, past associations

What Determines a Person's Weight?
- Set point: "Natural" body weight
  - Weight loss below a person's set point is often regained
  - Number of fat cells, metabolic rate may contribute to set point
- What causes obesity?
  - Biological and psychological factors contribute, including set point, eating habits, stress levels

_____

_____

_____

_____

_____

_____

_____

Eating Disorders: Anorexia Nervosa
- Condition in which an otherwise healthy person refuses to maintain a normal weight because of intense fear of overweight
- People with anorexia appear extremely thin
- Serious, chronic condition that can cause low blood pressure, loss of bone density, digestive problems, even death

_____

_____

_____

_____

_____

_____

Eating Disorders: Bulimia Nervosa
- Involves binge eating followed by purging (vomiting, laxative abuse)
- People with bulimia may appear to be of normal weight, unlike those with anorexia
  - Like those with anorexia, people with bulimia are fearful of weight gain
- Can lead to tooth decay, intestinal damage

_____

_____

_____

_____

_____

_____

What Causes Eating Disorders?

- Traditionally, cultural and media influences were blamed
- However, anorexia nervosa occurs all over the world, and has been documented for centuries
- By contrast, bulimia is more recent and is more limited to Western cultures

_____
_____
_____
_____
_____
_____
_____

Sexual Behavior: Learning Goals

- Describe the human sexual response cycle
- Consider the role of hormones in sexual behavior
- List external influences on sexual behavior
- Understand the factors that influence mate selection
- Discuss factors that may determine sexual orientation

_____
_____
_____
_____
_____
_____

The Sexual Response Cycle

- Documented by William Masters and Virginia Johnson (1966)
  - Studied physical responses during actual sexual encounters
- Four phases: excitement, plateau, orgasmic, resolution
- Highly similar in males and females
  - Exception: Most men experience an additional phase called the refractory period

_____
_____
_____
_____
_____
_____

Internal Influences: Hormones

- In most animals, sex hormones strongly determine sexual behavior
- In humans, sex hormones play some role, but a lesser one than in other animals
  - Example: Testosterone affects sexual desire in males and females
  - However: Sexual desire may persist after sex hormones decline (for example, after menopause)

External Factors

- Signals in the environment can stimulate sexual behavior
- Visual stimuli
- Touch
  - Erogenous zones
- Smell
  - Pheromones: Chemicals that stimulate sexual activity in animals; less effect on humans

Mate Selection

- Influenced by sociocultural factors such as sexual scripts
  - Example: Do you expect sex to lead to marriage?
- There may be evolutionary influences also, reflecting gender-specific adaptive problems
  - Example: Value placed on financial prospects (women) vs. attractiveness, youth (men)
  - Note that these behaviors are still flexible

Sexual Orientation
- A person's sexual, emotional attraction to members of the same sex or the other sex
- What factors determine sexual orientation?
    - Historically, psychologists believed that dysfunctional home environments led to homosexuality; this view no longer accepted
    - Likely some biological basis, but true causes still poorly understood

Expressing and Experiencing Emotion: Learning Goals
- Examine the evidence for and against basic emotions
- Understand the role of arousal in emotional experience
- Describe the subjective experiences of anger, happiness, and disgust
- Differentiate among the James-Lange, Cannon-Bard, and two-factor theories of emotion

Emotions
- Emotions are complex psychological events with several distinct components
    - Physiological (body) response, usually arousal
    - Expressive reaction, for example a facial expression
    - Subjective experience, such as a feeling
- Consider: What is the purpose of emotions?

Are There Basic Emotions?
- Think of all the terms used to describe emotions: Which are the basic ones?
- Certain facial expressions universally interpreted the same way, even in widely distant cultures (e.g., U.S. and rural New Guinea)
- Facial feedback hypothesis
- Could some complex emotions be blends of basic ones?

Arousal and Emotional Experience
- Emotions lead to physiological arousal
  - Increases in muscle tension, heart rate, pulse and blood pressure
- Arousal is adaptive in many situations
- Negative aspects of arousal:
  - Task performance reduced when it is too high (or too low)
  - Memory may be impaired

Subjective Experiences: Anger
- Everyone experiences anger from time to time
- Causes tend to involve expectations that are violated
- Is it healthy to express anger?
  - May feel calming
  - Physically expressing anger tends to lead to more such expressions in the future

Happiness
- Like anger, depends a great deal on expectations
  - Age, sex, race have little effect
- Often relative; we use current standard of living, past experience, other people as comparisons
  - Adaptation level
  - Large life changes often fail to cause long-term changes in happiness level

Disgust
- Aversion toward something distasteful
  - Typical expression: wrinkling nose, gaping mouth
- Relates to food choice, but is fairly complex
  - When an object touches something disgusting, it's considered "contaminated," even if sterilized
- Disgust is universal, but some triggers have to be learned

Theories of Emotion
- What's the relationship between our bodily reactions and our subjective experience?
  - Common sense suggests that the experience comes first, but psychologists disagree
- James-Lange theory: Body reactions come first; they drive the subjective experience of emotion
- Cannon-Bard theory: Body reactions happen together, but independently

The Two-Factor Theory

- The cognitive interpretation, or appraisal, of a body reaction drives the subjective experience of emotion
- Schacter and Singer: How you experience the effects of a drug that increases arousal (epinephrine) depends on your appraisal
  - Participants either led to expect effects of drug, or not
  - Interpreted their feelings of arousal as a function of drug, or other factors

Psychology For a Reason: Motivation and Emotion

- Activating Behavior
- Meeting Biological Needs: Hunger and Eating
- Meeting Biological Needs: Sexual Behavior
- Expressing and Experiencing Emotion

Chapter 12: Personality

_____

_____

_____

_____

_____

_____

_____

What Is Personality?
- Set of psychological characteristics that differentiates us from others and leads us to act consistently across situations
- Involves the study of individual differences in personality traits
  - Trait: Predisposition to respond in a certain way

_____

_____

_____

_____

_____

_____

What's It For? Personality
- Conceptualizing and Measuring Personality
- Determining Why Personality Develops
- Resolving the Person-Situation Debate

_____

_____

_____

_____

_____

_____

Conceptualizing and Measuring Personality: Learning Goals
- Discuss how factor analysis helps identify basic personality traits
- Distinguish among cardinal, central, and secondary traits
- Describe self-report inventories and projective personality tests

The Factor Analytic Approach
- Factor analysis: Mathematical procedure used to analyze correlations among test responses
  - Example: Asking people how well a particular term ("brooding," "friendly," etc.) describes them
- Main question: Which terms cluster together statistically?
  - Terms that go together probably reflect a general personality characteristic

Early Use of Factor Analysis
- The personality researcher Cattell used thousands of terms to establish the existence of 16 main personality traits
- Eysenck used a similar approach, but argued that there are really only 3 main factors
  - Called primary dimensions or superfactors
- Extroversion
- Neuroticism
- Psychoticism

The Big Five
- An intermediate between Cattell's fine-grained approach and Eysenck's general one
- Factor analysis approach in which there are 5 personality dimensions, including:
    - Extroversion
    - Agreeableness
    - Conscientiousness
    - Neuroticism
    - Openness

Allport's Trait Theory
- Focus is on individuals, not groups
- Personality described by a set of traits
    - Central traits: 5-10 descriptive traits that describe a person
    - Secondary traits: Less obvious characteristics that appear only under certain circumstances
- Some individuals have cardinal traits, "ruling passions" that dominate their lives and personalities

Personality Tests: Self-Report Inventories
- These ask people to answer groups of questions about how they typically think, act, and feel
    - Responses compared to averages compiled from prior test takers
- Main uses include hiring decisions, diagnosing psychological disorders
- Most widely used: MMPI (Minnesota Multiphasic Personality Inventory)

Projective Personality Tests
- Projective tests ask people to interpret unstructured or ambiguous stimuli
  - Assumption is that you "project" your personality into the interpretation
- Most widely used:
  - Rorschach: "Ink blots"
  - Thematic Apperception Test: Ambiguous pictures of people, situations

Which Kind of Test Is Better?
- Self-report tests are highly standardized, easy to score, reliable and valid, but their accuracy depends on the accuracy, honesty of the person taking the test
- Projective tests help people open up, talk about themselves, but interpretation of responses can vary widely across testers
- Most psychologists agree that self-report inventories are more reliable, but both kinds are widely used

Determining How Personality Develops: Learning Goals
- Describe Freud's psychodynamic theory of personality and mind
- Summarize and evaluate humanistic approaches to personality
- Describe social-cognitive theories of personality

Freud's Psychodynamic Approach

- Psychodynamic theory holds that much of behavior is governed by unconscious forces
- Mind is divided into three parts:
    - Conscious mind contains things that occupy one's current attention
    - Preconscious mind contains things that aren't currently in consciousness, but can be accessed
    - Unconscious mind contains memories, urges, and conflicts that are beyond awareness

Role of the Unconscious Mind

- Contains memories, urges that are forbidden or dangerous (more on this later)
    - These are kept from consciousness, but can still cause problems
- Dreams express contents of unconscious mind
    - Manifest content: What you remember
    - Latent content: True meaning

The Structure of Personality

- Id: Governed by inborn instinctual drives, especially those related to sex, aggression
    - Obeys the pleasure principle
- Superego: Motivates people to act in an ideal fashion, according to moral customs
    - Obeys the idealistic principle
- Ego: Induces people to act with reason and deliberation, conform to outside world
    - Obeys the reality principle

Defense Mechanisms
- Different parts of personality are in constant conflict, especially with regard to the id
  - Defense mechanisms ward off the resulting anxiety from these confrontations
- These are unconscious
- Often involve self-deception or replacing one urge with another

The Arsenal of Defense Mechanisms
- Denial
- Rationalization
- Projection
- Reaction formation
- Sublimation

Psychosexual Development
- Conflicts, memories, urges in unconscious mind come from experiences in childhood
  - Emerging sexuality, pleasure, is the focus of many stages of development
- Failure to move through a stage properly leads to fixation
  - Fixated individuals continue to act in ways appropriate for a much earlier stage

Stages of Psychosexual Development

- First year: Oral stage
  - Pleasure comes from sucking, putting things in mouth
  - Fixation at this stage can cause overeating, smoking, nail-biting
- Second year: Anal stage
  - Pleasure comes from retaining or passing feces
  - Fixation at this stage can cause excessive neatness or excessive messiness

Stages of Psychosexual Development, Continued...

- Ages 3 to 5: Phallic stage
  - Pleasure comes from self-stimulation of genitals
  - Fixation here can cause relationship, sexual problems; also Oedipus complex
- Ages 5 to puberty: Latency period
  - Sexual feelings suppressed
- Puberty to adulthood: Genital stage
  - Mature sexual relationships with opposite sex

Evaluating Psychodynamic Theory

- Extremely influential, but not accepted by many modern psychologists
- Criticisms:
  - Lack of scientific evidence
  - Over-reliance on case studies of disturbed individuals
  - Biased against women
- Freud attributed reports of sexual abuse to unconscious conflicts

Humanistic Approaches to Personality
- Focuses on people's unique capacity for choice, responsibility and growth
- Rogers: Personality comes from self-concept
    - Problems arise from incongruence between self-concept and experiences, "conditions of worth"
- Maslow: Personality reflects where you are in a hierarchy of needs
    - We all have a need for self-actualization
    - Problems arise from failure to satisfy needs

Evaluating Humanistic Theories
- Also influential
- Emphasis on personal choice, responsibility, free will balance Freud's ideas well
- Criticisms:
    - Hard to predict or explain why drive for growth, self-actualization are sometimes expressed and sometimes not
    - Depends too much on self-report
    - Too optimistic?

Social-Cognitive Approaches to Personality
- Experience, plus how people interpret experience, determine personality growth and development
- Rooted in the behaviorist tradition; emphasizes learned behaviors over innate ones
- Important concepts:
    - Locus of control
    - Self-efficacy
    - Reciprocal determinism

Evaluating Social-Cognitive Theories
- Idea that some personality traits are learned is widely accepted, as is the role of cognitive factors in learning
- Criticisms:
  - Over-emphasizes how a person responds in particular situations rather than on traits of person as a whole
  - Under-emphasizes biological, genetic factors in development

Resolving the Person-Situation Debate: Learning Goals
- Define the person-situation debate and discuss its components
- Discuss how genetic factors influence personality

The Person-Situation Debate
- Do people really behave consistently across situations, or is behavior just determined by the situation?
  - Evidence suggests there's more consistency within the same kind of situation, less across different situations
  - Self-monitoring is one determinant of consistency
- Most psychologists believe that personality and situation interact

Genetic Factors

- Are identical twins highly similar in personality, even when raised apart?
  - MMPI scores indicate higher degree of similarity between identical twins than between fraternal twins, irrespective of raising environment
- At least some traits genetically determined
  - However: How they are expressed may depend on environment

Psychology for a Reason: Personality

- Conceptualizing and Measuring Personality
- Determining Why Personality Develops
- Resolving the Person-Situation Debate

_____
_____
_____
_____
_____
_____

_____
_____
_____
_____
_____
_____

Chapter 13: Social Psychology

Chapter 13: Social Psychology

_____

_____

_____

_____

_____

_____

What's It For? Social Psychology
- Interpreting the Behavior of Others
- Behaving in the Presence of Others
- Establishing Relations with Others

_____

_____

_____

_____

_____

_____

_____

Social Cognition: Learning Goals
- Discuss how physical attractiveness, stereotypes, and social schemas influence our impressions of others
- Discuss how we attribute causality to the behavior of others, explaining our biases and errors
- Explain how attitudes are formed and changed

_____

_____

_____

_____

_____

_____

Person Perception
- Attractive people assumed to have more positive characteristics
  - This tendency cuts across cultures, age groups
- Social schemas: General knowledge structure in long-term memory, relating to social experiences or people
  - May be used to "categorize" others, guide how we treat them

Stereotypes
- Collection of beliefs and impressions held about a group and its members
  - Example: Racial and gender stereotypes
  - May be activated unconsciously
- Lead us to expect certain kinds of behavior from members of certain groups
  - Self-fulfilling prophecy effect
- Prejudice and discrimination can result from rigid application of negative beliefs about a group

Attribution Theory
- In social interactions, you must constantly try to understand the causes for behavior
  - Assigning a cause = Attribution
- Covariation model: What other events or factors were present when the behavior occurred?
  - Consistency
  - Distinctiveness
  - Consensus

Internal Versus External Attributions

- We may attribute a behavior to an external event or situation or to an internal personality trait or disposition
- Based partly on covariation
  - When consistency, distinctiveness and consensus are high, we make an external attribution
  - When consistency is high, but distinctivenss and consensus are low, we make an internal attribution

_____
_____
_____
_____
_____
_____

Errors and Biases in Attribution

- Fundamental attribution error: Tendency to overestimate the influence of internal personal factors, underestimate influence of situational factors
- Actor-observer effect: Tendency to attribute our own behavior to external sources, behavior of others to internal sources
  - But: We make internal attributions for own actions when they produce positive outcomes (self-serving bias)

_____
_____
_____
_____
_____
_____

Attitudes

- Positive or negative evaluation or belief held about something, which in turn affects one's behavior
  - Cognitive component
  - Affective component
  - Behavioral component
- Formed through experience and learning, including classical conditioning, instrumental conditioning, and observational learning

_____
_____
_____
_____
_____
_____

Elaboration Likelihood Model

- Proposes two routes to attitude change
  - Central route operates when people are motivated, focused on message
  - Peripheral route operates when people are either unmotivated or unable to process message
- Source characteristics such as attractiveness matter more for the peripheral route
- Advertisers tend to focus on peripheral route

Cognitive Dissonance

- Festinger and Carlsmith (1959): Subjects induced to act inconsistently with true feelings often changed those feelings
- Cognitive dissonance: Tension produced when people act in a way inconsistent with attitudes
  - Reduced by either changing behavior or changing beliefs
  - Influential idea, but hard to predict how people react to it

Self-Perception Theory

- Alternative to dissonance theory in which people use observations of own behavior as a basis for inferring their own beliefs
  - Example: If I told people a job was interesting, that must mean I like the job
- Two persuasion techniques based on this idea:
  - Foot-in-the-door
  - Lowball

Social Influence: Learning Goals

- Define and discuss social facilitation and interference
- Describe the bystander effect and diffusion of responsibility
- Describe how behavior changes in a group setting
- Discuss some aspects of group decision making
- Describe the Milgram experiment and discuss what it implies about the power of authority
- Discuss how culture affects social influence

Social Faciliation and Interference

- In the presence of others, we may experience:
    - Social facilitation: Performance enhanced
    - Social interference: Performance impaired
- Interacts with task difficulty
    - Others facilitate performance of easy tasks, but they hinder performance of difficult ones
    - May happen because presence of others raises arousal

Social Influences on Altruism

- Altruism: Acting in a way that shows unselfish concern for the welfare of others
    - Evolutionary explanation: Reciprocal altruism
- Bystander effect: Reluctance to come to someone's aid when others are present
    - Famous example: Kitty Genovese case
- Diffusion of responsibility: Allowing sense of responsibility to spread out among those present

The Power of the Group
- Social loafing: Tendency to put in less effort when working in a group than when working alone
  - May be connected to the bystander effect, diffusion of responsibility
- Deindividuation: Loss of individuality that comes from being in a group
  - Example: People might do things when in a large, rowdy group that they would never do alone
  - May also relate to diffusion of responsibility

Conformity
- Tendency to comply with the wishes of the group
  - Opinions, feelings, behaviors generally move toward the norm
- Can be extreme, as in Asch's (1951, 1955) studies:
  - Confederate subjects lied about easy visual judgments
  - Many participants conformed

Group Decision-Making
- Group polarization: Tendency for a group's dominant point of view to become stronger, more extreme with time
  - May relate to conformity, wish to be liked by other group members
- Groupthink: Tendency for members to become so interested in seeking consensus that they ignore, suppress, dissenting views
  - Can be countered by encouraging dissent, awareness of the tendency

The Power of Authority: Obedience
- Form of compliance that occurs when people respond to orders of an authority figure
- Milgram's (1963) experiment tested the predisposition of people to obey orders
    - Experimenter ordered participants to administer increasing levels of shock to an unwilling "victim"
    - IMPORTANT: "Victim" was a confederate; all shocks were fake

Results of the Milgram Experiment
- Over half delivered "shocks" up to the maximum level, despite realistic protests and screams of the "victim"
- Ethical concerns:
    - Participants clearly distressed
    - However, participants were debriefed, and long-term effects were minor
- What we learn from it: Under certain circumstances, average people will obey extreme orders

The Role of Culture
- Western cultures promote an independent view of the self
    - Leads to devaluing conformity, obedience, altruism
- Many non-Western cultures promote an interdependent view
    - Example: Japanese culture strongly emphasizes belonging to, contributing to a collective

Establishing Relations with Others: Learning Goals

- Describe the factors that influence our perception of facial attractiveness
- Explain the factors that influence us to like or love others
- Define the components of romantic love and explain the triangular theory

What Makes a Face Attractive?

- Evolutionary perspective: Attractiveness relates to how healthy a person is (and ultimately, to mate choice)
    - Example: Cultures agree somewhat on facial attractiveness
- Prototypicality: "Averaged" faces are especially attractive
- Subjective components: Cultural preferences, experience also affect attractiveness
    - Example: Attractiveness of pierced noses

Determinants of Liking and Loving

- Proximity: Likelihood of becoming friends strongly determined by how close by someone lives
- Similarity: Friends typically resemble each other
    - Example: social status, age, education, politics
- Reciprocity: Tendency to return in kind feelings that are shown toward us

139

What Is Romantic Love?
- Complex emotion expressed in a variety of ways
- Romantic love differs from other kinds, such as parent-child, friend-friend
- Two kinds of romantic love:
  - Passionate
  - Companionate

_____
_____
_____
_____
_____
_____
_____

The Triangular View of Love
- Sternberg (1986, 1999): Love is composed of three major dimensions
  - Intimacy
  - Passion
  - Commitment
- All forms can be defined in terms of these three dimensions
  - Example: Passionate love high on intimacy and passion, but low on commitment
- Dimensions develop differently over time

_____
_____
_____
_____
_____
_____

Psychology for a Reason: Social Psychology
- Interpreting the Behavior of Others
- Behaving in the Presence of Others
- Establishing Relations with Others

_____
_____
_____
_____
_____
_____

Chapter 14: Psychological Disorders

Chapter 14: Psychological Disorders

_____
_____
_____
_____
_____
_____
_____

What's It For? Psychological Disorders
- Conceptualizing abnormality
- Classifying psychological disorders
- Understanding psychological disorders

_____
_____
_____
_____
_____
_____
_____

Conceptualizing Abnormality: Learning Goals
- Evaluate the various criteria that have been used to define abnormality
- Discuss the legal definition of insanity
- Explain how the medical model classifies and categorizes abnormality
- Discuss the effects of diagnostic labeling

_____
_____
_____
_____
_____
_____

Characteristics of Abnormal Behavior
- Behavior must fit at least several of the following criteria to be labeled abnormal:
  - Statistical deviance
  - Cultural deviance
  - Emotional distress
  - Dysfunction
- "Abnormal" behavior not a rigid category

The Concept of Insanity
- Insanity: A legal term defined as inability to understand that certain actions are wrong at the time of a crime
  - Under this definition, people with disorders may be judged legally sane
- Famous cases in which the insanity defense succeeded: John Hinckley Jr., Jeffrey Dahmer
- Used in < 1% of criminal felony cases

Abnormality as a Disease: The Medical Model
- View that abnormal behavior is symptomatic of underlying "disease" that can be "cured" with appropriate therapy
  - Draws an analogy between mental and physical illness
- A widely held view, but some question it
  - Causes of mental illness often unclear
  - Social, cultural context of symptoms is important, more so than for physical illness

Problems Associated with Labeling

- Diagnostic labeling effects: Labels for psychological problems can become self-fulfilling prophecies
  - Make it difficult to recognize normal behavior when it occurs
  - May increase likelihood of abnormal behavior
- Rosenhan (1973): Participants faked disorders to enter psychiatric ward
  - Other patients saw through the deception, but staff did not

Classifying Psychological Disorders: Learning Goals

- Describe the DSM-IV-TR
- Describe the common anxiety disorders
- Describe the somatoform disorders
- Describe the common dissociative disorders
- Describe the common mood disorders
- Describe the characteristics of schizophrenia
- Describe the common personality disorders

What is the DSM-IV-TR?

- *Diagnostic and Statistical Manual of Mental Disorders, 4th edition–* Published by the American Psychiatric Association
- Used for the diagnosis and classification of psychological disorders
  - Intended to give objective, measurable criteria for diagnosing disorders
  - Does not suggest therapies or treatments
  - Does not discuss possible causes

The Five Axes of the DSM-IV-TR
- "Axis" = Rating dimension
  - Involve a wide range of factors including medical history, functioning in daily life
- Axis I: Common psychological disorders
  - Examples: Schizophrenia; substance abuse
- Axis II: Personality disorders
  - Example: Paranoid personality disorder

The Five Axes, continued...
- Axis III: General medical conditions
  - Example: Diseases of the circulatory system
- Axis IV: Psychosocial and environmental problems
  - Example: Homelessness
- Axis V: Global assessment of functioning scale

Anxiety Disorders
- Marked by excessive apprehension, worry that impairs normal functioning
  - Generalized anxiety disorder: "Free-floating" anxiety, chronic worrying lasting over 6 months
- Panic disorder: Recurrent discrete episodes or attacks of extremely intense fear or dread
  - Many physical symptoms such as chest pains
  - May be associated with agoraphobia (fear of public places)

Anxiety Disorders, Continued...
- Obsessive-compulsive disorder: Persistent, uncontrollable thoughts (obsessions) or compelling need to perform repetitive acts (compulsions)
    - Examples: Excessive cleaning, checking
- Specific phobia disorder: Highly focused fear of a specific object or situation
    - Example: Irrational fear of snakes

Somatoform Disorders
- Psychological disorders that focus on the physical body
- Hypochondriasis: Long-lasting preoccupation with idea that one has a serious disease, based on misinterpretation of normal body reactions
- Somatization disorder: Long-lasting preoccupation with body symptoms that have no physical cause
- Conversion disorder: Real physical problems that seem to have no physical cause

Dissociative Disorders
- Characterized by separation, or dissociation, of conscious awareness from previous thoughts or memories
- Dissociative amnesia: Inability to remember important personal information
    - Generally psychological in origin
- Dissociative fugue: Loss of personal identity, often accompanied by a flight from home

Dissociative Identity Disorder
- Individual alternates between what appear to be two or more distinct identities or personalities
  - Also known as multiple personality disorder
- Recognized by DSM-IV-TR, but not all clinicians believe in it
  - Some symptoms can be faked; others, such as optical changes, less easy to fake
  - Some clinicians view it as role-playing

Mood Disorders
- Prolonged, disabling disruptions in emotional state
- Bipolar disorder: Disordered mood shifts in two directions, from depression to manic state
  - Manic state: Person becomes hyperactive, talkative, decreased need for sleep
  - Manic state must last at least a week to be classified as such, but may last for months
  - Note that functioning is often severely impaired

Major Depressive Episode
- Five or more of these symptoms for at least 2 weeks:
  - Depressed mood for most of the day
  - Loss of interest in normal daily activities
  - Significant weight change
  - Change in activity level
  - Daily fatigue or loss of energy
  - Negative self-concept
  - Trouble concentrating or making decisions
  - Suicidal thoughts

Suicide
- One possible consequence of mood disorders, including bipolar disorder
  - Third leading cause of death among adolescents, eighth leading among all ages
  - Risk factors besides mood disorders include alcohol use, stressful events
- Another major predictor: Prior suicide attempts and thoughts
  - Suicidal thoughts are a serious warning sign

Schizophrenia
- Involves fundamental disturbances in thought processes, emotion, and/or behavior
- Complex disorder that may be expressed in a variety of ways
  - Diagnosis comes from a variety of symptoms

Schizophrenia
- Positive symptoms: Observable expressions of abnormal behavior
  - Hallucinations
  - Delusions
  - Disorganized speech
- Negative symptoms: Elimination or reduction of normal behavior
  - Flat affect: Little or no emotional reaction to events
  - Refusing to take care of self

Personality Disorders

- Chronic, enduring patterns of behavior leading to significant impairment in social functioning
  - Tendency to act inflexibly
- Examples:
  - Paranoid personality disorder
  - Dependent personality disorder
  - Antisocial personality disorder
- Some clinicians view these as extremes of personality rather than disorders per se

Understanding Psychological Disorders: Learning Goals

- Explain how biological and genetic factors can contribute to psychological disorders
- Discuss how maladaptive thoughts can contribute to psychological disorders
- Explain how environmental factors can contribute to psychological disorders

Biological Factors

- Include physical problems with the body, brain, as well as genetic influences
- Neurotransmitter imbalances:
  - Dopamine excess in schizophrenia
  - Serotonin involved in mood disorders, but exactly how is less clear
- Structural problems in the brain:
  - Schizophrenia associated with enlarged ventricles

Genetic Contributions

- Do some people inherit predispositions toward developing disorders?
- Genetic component of schizophrenia:
  - Likelihood of having it increases with closeness of a relative who also has it
  - Highest likelihood for identical twin (chances are 1 in 2)
- Similar pattern for depression, bipolar disorder

Cognitive Factors

- Maladaptive thought patterns may contribute
- Maladaptive attributions
  - Internal, stable, global attributions for negative experiences may play a role in depression
- Learned helplessness: Acquired when people repeatedly fail in attempts to control environment
  - May also contribute to depression

Environmental Factors

- Do people learn to act abnormally?
- Role of culture
  - A culture that emphasizes thinness may predispose you to anorexia nervosa
  - Cultural background may influence the kinds of delusions seen in schizophrenia
- Conditioning may play a role as well
  - Specific phobias may be acquired through classical conditioning or observational learning

149

Psychology for a Reason: Psychological Disorders

- Conceptualizing abnormality
- Classifying psychological disorders
- Understanding psychological disorders

_____

_____

_____

_____

_____

_____

_____

Chapter 15: Therapy

Chapter 15: Therapy

_____

_____

_____

_____

_____

_____

_____

What's It For? Therapy
- Treating the Body
- Treating the Mind
- Treating the Environment
- Evaluating and Choosing Psychotherapy

_____

_____

_____

_____

_____

_____

Biomedical Therapies: Learning Goals
- Explain how drug therapies are used to treat psychological disorders
- Discuss and evaluate electroconvulsive therapy
- Explain why psychosurgery is sometimes used to treat psychological disorders

_____

_____

_____

_____

_____

Drug Therapies

- Antipsychotic drugs reduce positive symptoms of schizophrenia
  - Chlorpromazine first used in 1950s to treat delusions, hallucinations
  - Most act on dopamine
  - Side effects include involuntary movements of tongue, jaw, face

_____

_____

_____

_____

_____

_____

Drug Therapies, Continued…

- Antidepressant drugs modulate availability or effectiveness of neurotransmitters implicated in mood disorders
  - Tricyclics modulate norepinephrine
  - Fluoxetine (Prozac) modulates serotonin
- SSRIs
- Lithium carbonate used for bipolar disorder
- Antianxiety drugs reduce tension, anxiety
  - Most act on gamma-aminobutyric acid (GABA)

_____

_____

_____

_____

_____

Electroconvulsive Therapy

- Brief electric shock delivered to the brain
  - Used mainly for depression
- Successful 50-70% of the time
- Often the treatment of "last resort"
  - Anesthesia, muscle relaxants reduce physical trauma
- Controversial because:
  - Unclear exactly how or why it works
  - Causes confusion, loss of memory
  - Relapse rate is high

_____

_____

_____

_____

_____

Psychosurgery
- Surgery that destroys or alters tissues in the brain in an effort to affect behavior
  - Exceedingly rare type of treatment
- Prefrontal lobotomy is the most famous example
  - Pioneered by Egas Moniz in 1930s
  - Produced calming effects, but also serious cognitive deficits, sometimes death
- Modern example: Cingulotomy
  - Used for severe obsessive-compulsive disorder, depression

Treating the Mind: Learning Goals
- Evaluate psychoanalysis as a form of therapy
- Evaluate cognitive therapies
- Evaluate humanistic therapies
- Discuss group and family therapies

Psychoanalysis
- Derived from Freud's work
- Goal: Bring hidden impulses, memories to surface of awareness
- Techniques:
  - Free association: Patient relaxes and freely expresses whatever comes to mind
  - Dream analysis: Determine latent content of dreams
- Resistance and transference usually happen

Contemporary Psychoanalysis

- Classical form of psychoanalysis is very lengthy and time-consuming
- Contemporary psychoanalysts often "streamline" or speed up the process
- May also tailor the process to particular needs of the patient, rather than address entire personality

Cognitive Therapies

- Goal: Remove irrational beliefs, negative thoughts presumed to be responsible for psychological disorders
  - Example: Depression
- Techniques:
  - Identify irrational beliefs, maladaptive interpretations of events
  - Challenge beliefs directly
  - Encourage more rational beliefs and interpretations

Rational-Emotive Therapy (Ellis)

- Therapist verbally assaults irrational thought processes almost like a cross-examiner
- Can be harsh and confrontational at times
- Examples of irrational beliefs:
  - "I must be loved and approved of by everyone"
  - "It's awful when things are not the way I would like them to be"

Beck's Cognitive Therapy
- Less harsh and confrontational than rational-emotive therapy
- Encourages clients to identify irrational thought processes themselves
  - Record keeping or "homework" is often used to pinpoint thought processes that lead to negative emotions

Humanistic Therapies
- Goal: Help clients gain insight into their fundamental self-worth, value as human beings
- Roger's client-centered therapy is the most common approach; others include:
  - Gestalt therapy
- "Empty-chair technique"
  - Existential therapies
- Focus on fundamental choices in life

Client-Centered Therapy
- Client, not therapist, holds the key to psychological health, happiness
- Problems stem from incongruence between self-concept, reality of everyday experiences
  - Others attach conditions of worth to approval, causing us to act inconsistently with true feelings

What Client-Centered Therapists Provide

- Genuineness: Therapist is not "phony," expresses feelings openly and honestly
- Unconditional positive regard: Therapist does not place conditions of worth on client
  - Accepts and respects client no matter how client behaves, no matter what client says
- Empathy: Therapist tries to see things from the client's perspective

Group Therapy

- Form of therapy in which several people are treated simultaneously in the same setting
- Advantages:
  - Cost effective
  - Can learn from others with similar issues
  - Can learn that you are not alone with psychological problems
- Special form: Family therapy
  - Attempts to treat family as a social system, improve communication and collaboration

Treating the Environment: Learning Goals

- Explain how conditioning techniques can be used in therapy
- Explain how rewards and punishments can be used in therapy

Conditioning Techniques

- Systematic desensitization: Use counterconditioning, extinction to reduce fear
- Work through an "anxiety hierarchy" of situations that lead to fearful reactions
- Imagine fearful situations while remaining relaxed
- Aversion therapy: Replace a positive reaction to a harmful stimulus with something negative
  - Example: Give a drug that causes severe nausea when alcohol is ingested

Applying Rewards and Punishments

- Token economies: Patients rewarded with small tokens when they act appropriately
  - Can exchange tokens for privileges
- Punishment: Follow an undesirable behavior with something aversive, or removing something pleasant
  - Example: Give mild shocks to a disturbed child to prevent self-destructive behavior
  - Note potential side effects, ethical concerns

Social Skills Training

- Uses modeling and reinforcement to shape appropriate adjustment skills
- For example, to teach conversational skills, the therapist might:
  - Discuss appropriate verbal responses
- May be followed with a videotaped demonstration
  - Role play a conversation
  - "Assign" client to practice skills before next session

Evaluating and Choosing Psychotherapy: Learning Goals

- Discuss the major findings of clinical evaluation research
- Describe the factors that are common across psychotherapies

Clinical Evaluation Research

- Clinical researchers contrasted effectiveness of different therapies for anxiety disorders
    - One group got psychodynamic therapy, another behavioral therapy, and control group remained on a waiting list
    - Both approaches produced improvement, but little differences between them
- Meta-analysis comparing many different studies found similar results

Controversies in Clinical Evaluation

- Control groups tend to improve too
    - "Spontaneous remission"
    - However: Does the support given while on waiting list produce improvement?
- Other research suggests that the effectiveness of therapy depends on the kind of problem
    - Cognitive therapies are best for depression, while behavioral therapies are best for some kinds of anxiety disorders

Common Factors Across Psychotherapies
- Support factors: Empathy, acceptance
- Learning factors: Feedback, new ideas
- Action factors: Specific suggestions for action
    - Example: Relaxation training

Psychology for a Reason: Therapy
- Treating the Body
- Treating the Mind
- Treating the Environment
- Evaluating and Choosing Psychotherapy

Chapter 16: Stress and Health

Chapter 16: Stress and Health

_____

_____

_____

_____

_____

_____

_____

What's It For? Stress and Health
- Experiencing Stress
- Reacting to Prolonged Stress
- Reducing and Coping with Stress
- Living a Healthy Lifestyle

_____

_____

_____

_____

_____

_____

_____

Experiencing Stress: Learning Goals
- Describe the stress response
- Explain the function of cognitive appraisal as part of the stress response
- Discuss external sources of stress
- Discuss internal sources of stress

_____

_____

_____

_____

_____

_____

The Stress Response

- Stress: Physical and psychological reactions to demanding situations
  - Stressors: The demanding or threatening situations that produce stress

_____

_____

_____

_____

_____

_____

_____

Physiological Reactions to Stress

- General Adaptation Syndrome (GAS)
- People react to threats in three stages:
  - Alarm: "Fight-or-flight" response; body energized
  - Resistance: Body adjusts to cope with the threat
  - Exhaustion: Energy depleted; body "gives up"
- Still influential, but modern research suggests that cognitive appraisal is important too

_____

_____

_____

_____

_____

_____

Psychological Reactions to Stress

- Emotional reactions may include fear, anger
  - Others include sadness, dejection, grief
- Is stress ever psychologically beneficial?
  - Possible benefits:
    - o Learning new skills
    - o Gaining confidence in one's problem-solving skills
  - May be important to have control and/or success in the stressful situation

_____

_____

_____

_____

_____

_____

Gender Differences
- Basic physiological response to stress does not differ
- Some predisposition for females to react differently than males
  - "Tend and befriend" strategy
  - May reflect evolutionary pressures to protect offspring, maintain social network
- Controversial idea, however
  - Note that females can and do show aggression under certain circumstances

Cognitive Appraisal
- In order to feel stress, you need to:
  - Perceive a threat
  - Conclude that you may not have the resources to deal with the threat
- Example: Everyone in a class gets the same test, but not everyone feels the same threat
  - Stress lessened if:
    - o Test seen as easy (demanding)
    - o Test seen as unimportant

External Sources of Stress: Significant Life Events
- Changes that disrupt everyday life
  - Even positive events such as holidays and vacations can cause some stress
- Holmes and Rahe (1967) ranked the stressfulness of different life events
  - Examples: Death of spouse = 100; vacation = 13
- Some studies demonstrate a connection between significant life events, physical and psychological problems

Other External Sources of Stress

- Daily hassles: Small daily problems and irritations "add up" in terms of stress
  - Examples: Traffic, long lines
- Environmental factors:
  - Chronic exposure to noise increases stress, stress-related issues
  - Crowding increases stress and aggression
  - Environmental psychology: Specialty area devoted to study of environmental effects on behavior and health

Internal Sources of Stress

- Perceived control: Amount of influence you feel you have over a situation, your reaction
  - More perceived control -> Less stress
- Explanatory style
  - Internal, stable, global attributions -> More stress
- Personality characteristics
  - Optimistic, "Type B" people experience fewer stress-related ailments than hard-driving "Type A" people

Reacting to Prolonged Stress: Learning Goals

- Describe the physical consequences of prolonged stress
- Describe the psychological consequences of prolonged stress

Physical Consequences of Prolonged Stress

- Immune system response lowered
  - Can be measured by counting the number of lymphocytes (white blood cells)
  - Affects likelihood of contracting cold / flu viruses
  - May affect cancer likelihood as well, but this link is controversial
- Cardiovascular system affected
  - Increased blood pressure
  - Increased cholesterol levels in the blood

Psychological Consequences of Prolonged Stress

- Posttraumatic stress disorder: Flashbacks, avoidance of stimuli associated with the traumatic event, and chronic arousal
  - Relatively rare
- Burnout: Physical, emotional, and mental exhaustion created by long-term involvement in an emotionally demanding situation
  - More common in people who approach stressful jobs with a strong sense of idealism

Reducing and Coping with Stress: Learning Goals

- Explain how relaxation techniques can be used to reduce stress
- Explain how stress can be managed through cognitive reappraisal of the stressful situation

Relaxation Techniques
- Progressive muscle relaxation: Concentrate on relaxing specific muscle groups in a set order
- Autogenic relaxation: Focus on directing blood flow toward tense muscle groups to "warm" them
- Meditation: Muscle relaxation, plus mental exercises to help reduce stress-producing thoughts

Another Technique: Biofeedback
- Specific physiological feedback that people are given about the effectiveness of their relaxation efforts
  - Example: Instruct headache sufferers to relax forehead muscles; give feedback about tension in that area
- Does tend to reduce stress-related tension and pain
  - May result from increasing perceived control

Social Support
- Resources that individuals receive from other people or groups, often in the form of comfort, caring, or help
  - These improve psychological and physical health by reducing stress
- Why does it work?
  - Friends/family encourage healthy lifestyle, bolster confidence
  - "Opening up" helps reduce stress
- Writing in a journal produces similar results as talking to a friend

Reappraising the Situation
- Recall that it's our interpretation of events, not events themselves, that produce stress
  - Example: A change of plans can be seen as a welcome break or as a terrible catastrophe
- Ways to reduce stress through reappraisal:
  - Distract self from "catastrophizing"
  - Keep a record of stress-producing situations, analyze your reactions

Living a Healthy Lifestyle: Learning Goals
- Discuss the physical and psychological benefits of aerobic exercise
- Discuss the consequences of tobacco use and explain why quitting smoking is so difficult
- Discuss the value of proper nutrition
- Describe the different types of prevention programs and explain how they're used to target AIDS

Aerobic Exercise
- High-intensity activities that increase heart rate, oxygen consumption
  - Examples: Running, swimming
- Positive effects:
  - Increases lifespan
  - Improves cardiovascular function
  - Improves mood, resistance to stress and depression
- Exact reason why is unknown, however

Avoiding Tobacco
- Vast majority of researchers agree that smoking is addictive, dangerous
  - Health consequences include heart disease, cancer, and stroke
- Why people smoke anyway:
  - Chemical effect on the brain is highly reinforcing
  - Advertising associates smoking with independence, nonconformity
  - Nicotine withdrawal is unpleasant

_____

_____

_____

_____

_____

_____

Proper Nutrition
- Overwhelming amount of evidence links quality of diet to health, length of life
- Why people eat poor diets anyway:
  - Psychological factors lead to poor food choices
  - Many unhealthy food choices are highly reinforcing
- Example: French fries are more reinforcing than a baked potato

_____

_____

_____

_____

_____

_____

Prevention and Health
- Three main approaches:
  - Primary prevention: Educate public about ways to prevent a problem before it starts
  - Secondary prevention: Early identification of risk factors in specific population groups
  - Tertiary prevention: Handle and contain an illness once it has been acquired
- All three are valuable, but primary prevention has the greatest long-term value

_____

_____

_____

_____

_____

_____

AIDS and Prevention

- Acquired immunodeficiency syndrome, resulting from HIV
  - Gradually weakens and disables the immune system
- All three prevention approaches are useful for fighting AIDS
- Psychologists' special role:
  - Educate public about transmission and counter misinformation
  - Help reduce stress in HIV-positive people

_____

_____

_____

_____

_____

_____

Steps for Preventing HIV Transmission

- Contact with bodily fluids transmits HIV
  - Includes saliva, urine, and tears, but blood and semen are much more likely means for transmission
- Two main routes of contact: Sharing intravenous needles and sexual contact
  - Use of latex condoms during sex drastically reduces chances of infection

_____

_____

_____

_____

_____

_____

Psychology For a Reason: Stress and Health

- Experiencing Stress
- Reacting to Prolonged Stress
- Reducing and Coping with Stress
- Living a Healthy Lifestyle

_____

_____

_____

_____

_____

_____

_____

_____